*"**The Young Adult Writer's Journey**" is a 'Must Have' at your fingertip reference for anyone who writes (or wants to write) for or about kids. Engaging text with topical and thought-provoking insights leading from idea to submission and beyond to populate a story with believable characters young readers can relate to."—Nancy Gideon, Award-Winning author of the By Moonlight series*

The Young Adult Writer's Journey

An Encyclopedia for Y A Writers

Janet Schrader-Post & Elizabeth Fortin-Hinds

Printed in the United States of America

To Laylany for her expert help, and all the other wonderful, complex teenagers everywhere....

Table of Contents

Genre and Structure

Chapter One

Who's Reading Young Adult Fiction, and Why?

Great YA books and New Adult fiction have created an audience of adult readers as well as teens. Fifty-five percent of the readers of YA fiction aren't teens, they're adults. Statistics say they're in the eighteen to thirty-year-old category, but many readers are much older. Some find them relaxing, the characters charming and funny, the situations reminiscent of their own childhood dreams of beating the odds, defying their parents, and overcoming the hardships of growing up. Who doesn't love seeing kids succeed?

The period in a person's life between thirteen and twenty is the hardest. Teens grow physically. Their bodies go through crazy changes they must deal with every day while navigating school, athletics, and learning to socialize. They're under the gun from teachers, parents and most importantly, from their peers. Many of them crash and burn. A kid can totally ruin his or her entire life before age fifteen.

To write successfully about teens you must understand them. They are often a misunderstood group. They are maligned for acting out or being rude and disobedient. The complex nature of a teenager's life should be taken into consideration when writing for modern teens. Teen suicide rates are high. There are many reasons and many risk factors. Teenagers are prone to depression. Family life is not what it was in the fifties. In most homes, both parents work--if there even are two parents in the home. Divorce and single parent homes affect kids in a multitude of ways too.

The American Society for the Positive Care of Children list substance abuse, physical, mental and sexual abuse in the home as just some of the reasons for teen suicide. A family history of suicide and exposure to the suicidal behavior of peers can also affect teens. Kids in our times do not live in *Leave it to Beaver* or *Happy Days*. They struggle, they fight, and many succeed against terrible odds. This could be one of the reasons books with more mature themes, themes that reflect the struggles of teens in today's world, are popular.

Coming of age books used to be the main offering in the YA market, and it still applies. Kids still come of age, no matter what century it is. They just face different issues and overcome different obstacles. Learning as you go, making mistakes and making better choices, is what coming of age is all about. Teenagers have an exhausting and chaotic number of first times to deal with, all while juggling friends, family, school and...wait for it...social media. Self-esteem and trying to figure out who they are, who they should be, who they want to be and why are huge issues for them. Trying to be different while deeply concerned with fitting in and finding their niche in their world is huge for kids, and especially tough because they want everyone to believe they could care less. They drive themselves and often their parents to distraction finding just the right outfit, the one that looks as though they've thrown it on casually and just happen to look fantastic and trendy. Other kids might struggle to find a shirt that isn't ripped or missing buttons, or one that wasn't underneath a urine-soaked garment from one of their siblings.

Coming of age may still be a recurring theme in YA, but most readers don't think about it like that, probably because they're living it. No matter how old they are, humans perpetually come of age, from one life stage to the next. All main characters should demonstrate growth and change. You can find literature like that in fantasy, science fiction, urban fantasy, and other genres, but in YA, the protagonist is always a teenager. And following a kid through adventures, watching him or her develop skills and courage he or she never knew he or she had is what makes YA magical.

Not all kids read, but some devour books and read by flashlight under their covers. They hunt for books that excite them and interest them in ways video games can't compete with.

Characters in Young Adult fiction are what truly matter to the story itself. The teens and adults who read it want to laugh and cry with the characters the writer dreams up. Adults want to remember what it was like to be young, to be reminded of how hard they struggled and how much they have already overcome. Teens won't be interested in characters who aren't authentic either, who don't act and feel like either themselves or kids they know or want to know. And they all identify with how hard it is to be a teenager. They want to revisit or feel what it's like to be on the cusp of life, standing on the edge of their future, where all things are possible, and everything is fresh, new and exciting.

Teens who read want to connect with your characters, understand them, and feel what they feel. To make the characters real, you need to do more than read Young Adult fiction. You need to know the teens you're writing about. If you don't have any living with you, find a friend who does and talk to them and talk to their kids. It's not enough to just remember what your life as a teenager was like. You need to know what life as a teenager now is like, because the characters you create to engage young readers had better be real. They must be believable as teens, not adults disguised in teenager bodies. Teenagers are a lot smarter than you think. They will know if you try to fool them, so be careful and make sure the characters you create are not only fun and engaging, but real.

Some books about writing for teens list rules. Many of the most popular YA books throw the rules out from page one. Agents and publishers are searching for the next new *Hunger Games* or *Diary of a Wimpy Kid*--the hit potential, not a duplication of the tropes, mind you. They have open minds and may look at the new and crazy for just those reasons, so don't be afraid to experiment.

It's not enough to read a stack of YA books. Pick one you like and deconstruct it to figure out why it worked, why it's popular. Writing YA is fun because you can write anything you can imagine and are even encouraged to do so, if your characters are authentic teens with credible and real problems.

Teenagers make wonderful characters to write about. They are often more uninhibited than adults, braver, more impulsive. Those characteristics can get them into trouble and out of it just as fast. They can be very judgmental and equally self-conscious, hard on each other and themselves. They need guidance, but often won't listen to it. They fall in love easily, will do anything for those they love, and can show deep compassion for those weaker than themselves. These contradictions are reflected in all great young adult fiction. Katniss Everdeen was so brave in *Hunger Games*, she offered herself as tribute to save her sister. Teenagers are impulsive. Mare, in *The Red Queen*, is very hard on herself. She blames herself for her sister's injury. But when faced with a new world, an outrageous situation, she's brave and resourceful, accepts her new world, but still remembers those at home she loves.

When you write for young adults, you can think outside the box. Providing excitement in every page is required. YA readers want immediate gratification. They like complex plots, but they do want action all the way, and are impatient with plots that develop too slowly.

Maintaining the interest of kids bombarded with video games, Instagram, Snapchat, phone apps, a computerized, digitized, tweet-filled world, is the name of the game. If you want to play, better bring your A game because YA is so popular even famous authors like John Sanford, James Rollins, Stephen King and James Patterson have dipped their feet into the water. The competition is fierce, but the payoff is twofold; in the writing itself, which is a blast, and participating in the current big money market is never a bad idea.

People, old and young, read YA because many young adult novels are surprisingly good. Most people didn't expect young adult literature to have well-developed characters, complex plots, and great writing until the *Harry Potter* stories broke the mold. Today, they must be filled with inventive stories, great writing, and some of the best literary characters ever invented--characters that capture people's imaginations like Harry Potter, Katniss Everdeen and Stanley Yelnats IV from *Holes*. Great worlds are created in YA, worlds filled with crazy creatures, worlds that give its characters special powers we all wish we had, or worlds that are dark and dangerous that make us realize how lucky we are.

Young people are fun, because they are energetic, risk-takers, fearful of the many things they have yet to experience, but have a great thirst for exploration, discovery, and have that youthful self-deception that they are immortal.

There are poor kids from dysfunctional homes playing four sports, gaining notoriety, garnering awards, and winning scholarships. Teens are always struggling to become someone, to be successful in a rough environment. Think of movies like *The Big Green, The Perfect Game, Hardball,* or *The Blind Side,* where down and out and against all odds makes for great story.

School is not for sissies either. You recall that a kid can completely ruin his or her life in a single moment, with one bad choice. There are many examples. A teenage girl can get pregnant and drop out of school. Sometimes her boyfriend drops out to go to work, and sometimes she doesn't have a boyfriend. *Push* by Sapphire, which became the movie *Precious,* comes to mind or *Speak* by Laurie Halse Anderson. They tackle some very harsh realities, incest and rape. Date rape is very common and when three of four women will be raped, according to statistics, awareness of sexual predators isn't an uncommon topic for books that teens will want to read.

Sex, drugs and rock-n-roll is what they used to say. The phrase is still true. The music changes with each generation. Sex is more prevalent and dangerous, with diseases that can kill you. Drugs are readily available, and more lethal than ever. If kids don't die or become addicts, they can get in trouble with the law. With young kids committing adult crimes, they are often tried as adults these days, with adult consequences. These kids may like to escape in a carefree, sunny story, but more often they are looking for characters they can relate to, ones that have real problems and struggle to find solutions.

Teens walk a tightrope between depression, the aggression of bullies, the hard work of studying, pressure from parents to do too much, and all of this is liberally salted with a heavy dose of raging hormones. It's the best years of their lives for some and the end of their lives for too many.

There is nothing simple about modern-day teens. They are internet savvy. They know more about the workings of an iPhone® than most every adult. They understand *Snapchat*, Twitter, Instagram and they play complicated video games. They even read books on their phone and the two million copies of Hooked, an iPhone app that serves up thrillers for 13–24-year-olds via SMS conversations, prove it. Through the internet, they can talk to friends on Facebook, through chat rooms, and even on the computer video games they play. Teens of today are more informed and world-wise than many adults. Remember this when you write for them.

These savvy, world-wise kids navigate through metal detectors, under the eyes of countless security cameras and personnel, and the hallways of schools prepared to be locked-down to prevent mass shootings. They live with the knowledge that school-shootings exist, and friends and schoolmates, and even they themselves, are possible targets of the next one.

Teenagers are brave, fearless, and smart. They are more politically knowledgeable than you imagine. Books like *The Red Queen* by Victoria Aveyard and *The Hunger Games* by Suzanne Collins all include complex political situations just as the *Divergent* series by Veronica Roth does. The authors understood the interest young adult readers and adult readers have in politics and world order. They have genuine fear that we will have to fight for survival in the not-too-distant future like in *The 5ᵗʰ Wave* by Rick Yancey.

During the time they enter middle school and graduate from high school, their bodies undergo a complete transformation. Some of them discover they are not Barbie. It's not a pleasant discovery. Kids come in all sizes, shapes, and intelligence levels. So should your characters.

If you can look at these kids, see their struggles, and not love them, don't write YA. Stick with whatever you write now or choose something else. Don't jump into this genre because it's hot and trendy. Knowing and caring about teens is the most important part of writing YA. If you don't convince your readers that your teen protagonist is real, your book won't get read.

This is your target audience.

Get to know them.

Chapter Two

The Young Adult Technique

Writing can begin with only one idea. Harry Potter author, J.K. Rowling said, "All of a sudden the idea for Harry just appeared in my mind's eye. I can't tell you why or what triggered it. But I saw the idea of Harry and the wizard school very plainly. I suddenly had this basic idea of a boy who didn't know who he was, who didn't know he was a wizard until he got his invitation to wizard school. I have never been so excited by an idea." If you get an idea like that, go with it, but to engage the interest of young adults, there are a couple of tried and true techniques even Rowling stuck with.

Genre fiction has tropes. You can manipulate them, but readers of genre fiction expect certain thematic norms. Stephen King has a technique for writing horror novels that scare adults. He puts children and pets into jeopardy and proves to you that he will kill them. This scares the heck out of adults.

Young people tend to be rebellious. They often don't like authority. So, plot device one for creating YA fiction kids will love is to create an authority figure kids will love to hate.

Rowling created the Dursleys. Every kid who picked up the *Harry Potter* stories immediately loathed the Dursleys. It doesn't hurt to toss in a bully or two like cousin Dudley. I mean, who didn't cheer when Hagrid gave Dudley a pig's tail?

There isn't a teen out there who hasn't been bullied. It's one of the most common problems they face on a tough journey through modern-day school. Middle school is where it escalates. Kids are so terrified of being bullied they are thrilled to have even one best friend, cousin, or neighbor to hang with.

Middle school is a frightening place. Sixth-graders are wild. It's an odd moment in a child's life, sixth grade. They get their first taste of freedom and they run with it. Changing classes becomes an opportunity for some, and terrifying for others. Ever hear of a kid wearing three pairs of boxer shorts to school? In the first week of sixth grade, their favorite pastime is often pantsing each other.

Kids in middle school run the gamut from three-feet tall to six-five with a full beard. The three years between sixth and eighth grade can bring on some crazy physical and mental changes. This is where a kid can learn being a bully will get you everywhere, while on the other end of the spectrum, weaker kids are learning survival skills. It's rough being in middle school.

Adults can scare children too, and they can be anyone in their lives. One fantastic nasty character in a YA movie is Miss Trunchbull in *Matilda*. She was horrible, but wonderful, a headmistress from hell. Every child on the planet who saw that movie hated her. Cruella DeVil in *A Hundred and One Dalmatians* was epic. Darth Vader, James, the master of the hunt in *Twilight*, President Snow in *Hunger Games*, Jeanine Matthews, the leader of the Erudite in *Divergent*, and the list goes on. Create a character that teens will love to hate. It's the key to a successful YA story.

Villains are great characters, and the more complex the better. Give your bad guy a great backstory so they have a reason for being evil. You can't just make someone bad. Even crazy people have motivation for what they do. Their reasons are just crazy. Create a bad guy as wonderful as Dexter, as detailed as Darth Vader, as fun to hate as Miss Trunchbull.

Bad guys are one of the eight most common archetypes. They are shadows and don't even have to be seen to be frightening. In *Harry Potter and the Sorcerer's Stone*, no one sees Voldemort, but he exists as a terrible villain who is so frightening, his name can't be spoken. Shadows/villains exist to create threat and conflict, and to give the hero something to struggle against. Like many of the other archetypes, shadows do not have to be characters specifically – the dark side of the force is just as much a shadow for Luke in *Star Wars* as Darth Vader.

The second part of the formula is so obvious it just might not be. You need peers for your kid characters. They fill two roles. Peers are so important in young adult fiction it cannot be overstated. Teens rely on their friends for support through the rigorous trials of middle and high school. Without their friends, many fifteen-year-olds would wither and die. Their phone is connected to them. Even if they have support at home, it's not enough. They need these friends to help fight off the evil bullies infesting the halls of every school. They need them to prop up their flagging self-confidence. Peers and friends are another common archetype, allies. Every hero needs help, someone to watch the hero's back, carry the backpack or provide a much-needed skill the hero doesn't possess.

These peers can also play other archetypal roles besides the role of ally. Peers can be tricksters and mentors helping them navigate the dangers of the world of adventure or even the halls of high school. Peers who are allies can be shapeshifters when they suddenly turn into enemies. Remember Gollum in *The Lord of the Rings*?

Bullies in schools fall into many categories, the jocks, the pretty girls, the thugs, and often those who are being abused elsewhere. They hold their own power in schools and intend to keep it by putting others down and fueling their insecurities. Every teen is already a boiling mass of insecurities. Friends, peer groups, their own amazing inner strength, and the occasional helpful teacher hold them together.

One memorable bully in movies is Scott Farkus from *A Christmas Story*. He had red hair, freckles and a crummy toady. He made Ralphie and his friends' life hell. There are lots of bullies we loved to hate. Biff from *Back to the Future*, Regina George in *Mean Girls,* even a book/movie with as many outside conflicts as *The Maze Runner* had a bully. Gally tries to keep Thomas from entering the maze and saving all of them. In the end, Gally even kills Thomas's friend, Chuck. Gally was the epitome of a bully every teen could hate.

Bullies aren't always enemies. They don't often fit into the archetypical role of the shadow. Bullies can be heralds, announcing a need or situation the hero must face. They can be tricksters, adding humor to a serious situation, or they can be shapeshifters if they leave the dark side and come over to the hero's side. Bullies make great characters. Have fun creating them. Make them useful.

So, you've created a bad guy. You've got your villains down, your bully ready to go, now you need another part of the formula, friends.

Every teen has some friends. Even the loners, the introverts, the oddballs, seek the company of other kids like themselves. A common formula that works well in YA is the threesome. In the *Harry Potter* stories, had the iconic Hermione, Harry, and Ron threesome. In *The Hunger Games*, there was the Katniss, Peeta, Gale threesome. Even though Gale and Peeta competed for Katniss, they were still a threesome just like in *Twilight*, Bella, Edward and Jacob were a threesome. In the *Percy Jackson* stories, Percy, Annabeth Chase and Grover Underwood formed a threesome and in *Eragon*, Brom and Arya supported Eragon. It's a formula that works with teens as the threesome, but it can also work if you add an adult into the mix like the *Race to Witch Mountain* movie. The Rock played Jack Bruno who helped Seth and Sara.

Even though the threesome is a good formula, sometimes you need more men on your team. Teams are also a good way to bolster your protagonist. Everyone wants to be part of a team. School teaches kids playing on a team can build your confidence and provide you with friends. Teams work in young adult fiction the same way.

In *The Maze Runner*, Thomas had his team with him when he entered the maze to fight the Grievers. In *Jumanji: Welcome to the Jungle*, a team went into the game to save Jumanji. *Holes* and *Miss Peregrine's Home for Peculiar Children* used the team formula.

Although the threesome formula and the team formula work, most YA novels begin with a single protagonist, a hero or a heroine. Like Harry Potter, Bella, and Katniss, they all started their journey alone and picked up team members as they launched themselves into the world of their adventure. Your protagonist plays the hero archetype. He's the one who leads us into the world of adventure. He's in charge. Be careful not to make him too stereotypical. Teens love heroes they can relate to.

Once you've developed your awesome protagonist completely, created a villain everyone will love to hate, it's time to decide whether you're going to go with a character-driven story or plot your story out in detail and insert your characters into it. Writers have names for this--being a plotter or a pantser. Will you let the characters take you where they will, plotting by the seat of your pants, or be more in control, diagraming your plot first?

Maybe you're in the middle. You might like to have a synopsis based on The Hero's Journey to guide you, but you always create characters first, develop them as deeply and completely as you can, and sometimes, if you do it right, the characters will talk to you and lead you through your book. The feeling you get when you're running with what your characters are telling you to do is like no other.

Whichever way you decide to go, you develop a YA story by giving your protagonist a problem to solve, a quest, or a grave situation that needs to be resolved. Keep in mind as you create this problem that it needs to be something young people, teens, can relate to.

Another important element in many YA stories is romance. It's part of the formula. Every kid out there is worrying about their love life. It starts in sixth grade with a first crush and never ends. Teens are romantics by nature and in their hearts, they want to see two people fall in love. LGBT characters have become acceptable in YA fiction. Although some parents may try to shelter their kids from anyone they see as different, their kids don't exist in a vacuum. Kids see lesbians, gays, bisexuals and transgender peers in school, at the mall, and on TV all the time. They may be open about it, or they may still be trying to figure out their own sexuality. Kids in different schools react to non-heterosexuals in various ways. They may ignore it, shun them, mock them, shame them, or even harm them. There's a lot of story to be had there. Teenagers are hypersensitive about their sexuality. Even YA fiction that skirts intimacy can't ignore romance. Harry Potter had his crushes.

Many successful YA series have been written around romance and romantic conflict. *Twilight* has Bella, Jacob and Edward, *The Hunger Games* has Gale, Peeta and Katniss. In the *Upside of Unrequited* by Becky Albertelli, insecure Molly Peskin-Suso has twenty-six unrequited crushes. The characters in your YA don't have to be perfect. *The Fault in Our Stars* by John Green, where two kids fighting cancer fall in love, is a great example. Another example is *The DUFF* by Kody Keplinger. DUFF stands for designated ugly fat friend. The protagonist doesn't know she is a DUFF. Her success as she figures it out and overcomes the designation, makes you cheer. Growing up is hard, and for teens, falling in love, sometimes repeatedly, is part of it.

There are YA stories out there that don't have romantic elements. *Holes* pops into mind immediately, but the overwhelming majority of YA fiction and YA movies does.

To wrap up the formula for writing YA, you take a bad villain, add a quirky, compelling protagonist, toss in a huge problem, stir in two or three original team members, embark on an adventure, solve a big problem, mix in a little romance, and bring it to a satisfying conclusion.

Easy, right?

It is certainly less daunting if you let archetypes inform your character choices and development.

Chapter Three

Mythic Structure for Young Adult Novels

Most writing classes for Young Adult fiction and Middle Grade tell you the duty of your book's opening is to hook your reader and to catch the interest of an agent. The truth is, that's only one of the purposes of your opening. Too often we forget that, as Frank Herbert said in *Dune*, "A beginning is a very delicate time."

When writing for young adults, you should know where you're going, just as when you write adult fiction. Plot construction for stories with universal themes is the same in any genre. There is a plan, a plot, a diagram you can follow to create a satisfying read. Just as with painting, every artist who uses the same subject will create a different and unique work of art. So, using a basic outline to be sure you write a story that resonates to the inner psyche of readers is not a bad idea.

Some may argue that modern stories can't demonstrate enough diversity when trying to fit the entire world into a single format such as The Hero's Journey, but iconic success stories like *Star Wars*, *The Lord of the Rings*, the *Harry Potter* stories and more don't seem to mind. They're hardly the same stories, are they? Do they seem like boring knockoffs to you? Millions of fans and dollars later...they are still growing their fan base. Lucas even spoke of *Star Wars* and the incorporation of Joseph Campbell's Hero's Journey and appeared in his Bill Moyer's series.

Joseph Campbell was a professor of literature at Sarah Lawrence College, where he worked in comparative mythology and religious studies. He was strongly influenced by Carl Jung's view of myth. In his 1949 work *The Hero with a Thousand Faces*, Campbell described the basic mythic structure as follows:

A hero ventures forth from the world of common day into a region of supernatural

wonder: fabulous forces are there encountered, and a decisive victory is won: the

hero comes back from this mysterious adventure with the power to bestow boons

on his fellow man. (Campbell, Joseph (1949). <u>The Hero with a Thousand Faces</u>.

Princeton: <u>Princeton University Press</u>. p. 23.)

His iconic classic deconstructs universal story patterns. In his study of the myth of the hero, Campbell posits the existence of a Monomyth (a word he borrowed from James Joyce), a universal pattern, structure, found in heroic tales in every culture. While outlining the basic stages of this mythic cycle, he also explores common variations in the hero's journey, which, he argues, is an operative metaphor, not only for an individual, but for a culture as well. Although the stories may vary to suit the needs and beliefs of a specific culture, the underlying universal archetypes remain.

Christopher Vogler used this hero's journey to write, *The Writers Journey: Mythic Structure for Writers*. He simplified Campbell's 17 steps into 12, handy in today's 12-step minded society. What he did that was fantastic is make it more accessible for modern writers, who are not always scholars. There are several similar editions, including one for screenwriters. Women like Maureen Murdock have written books specifically about *The Heroine's Journey*. Although the steps may vary, the universal pattern, used in a novel or screenplay, creates a story with themes that resonate across cultures. It is so powerful, creating hit after hit, that it was required reading for Disney executives, a company that knows the importance of creating a hero's journey to appeal to mass audiences. Using this pattern to construct books in Young Adult novels provides the reader with a satisfying experience.

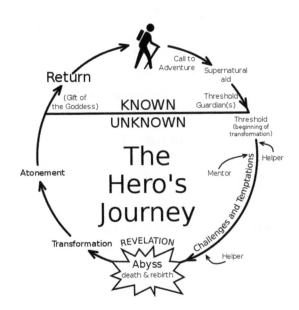

To illustrate the hero's journey, it's easier to understand in the context of a classic young adult book/movie, such as *Harry Potter*, already used to illustrate points throughout this book. It will be broken down for you according to the different stages in *The Hero's Journey*, with particular attention to how the journey relates to a YA hero/heroine, the focus of this entire book. Following are some things you need to think of before you sit down to write your first scene.

DEPARTURE

1.   *The Call to Adventure*

When a hero/heroine receives a call to adventure, it's important to let the reader in on the place from which they will begin their journey. Often, it helps the reader realize either how important the journey is or why the decision to embark on the journey is so difficult, such a strange and frightening proposal. The hero/heroine starts out in what both Campbell and Vogler call the Ordinary World. The Ordinary World allows us to get to know the hero/heroine before he/she sets out on their journey. Your story should start out in your hero or heroine's ordinary world, the place they live in every day. Even if your hero stays physically in the same place, you must make the Special World, even a figurative one, feel different. It should have a different tone, different rhythm and different priorities. In the Special World things are more dangerous, there is more at stake and the cost of a mistake is always higher.

Harry Potter begins in his home with the Dursleys who are amazingly ordinary and not very nice to poor Harry. Harry doesn't fit in. He lives under the stairs, which could be seen as an implied reference to servants in historical England who lived "below stairs." In the world of the Dursleys, Harry's a first-class outcast with a side order of whacko. He talks to snakes, his hair refuses to be cut, and, as Uncle

Vernon ominously implies, strange things happen whenever he's around.

You know from the very first scene where Dumbledore and McGonagall drop him on the Dursley doorstep, that he doesn't belong to their world. As a reader, you feel as though Harry is only in this world temporarily, and you can't wait to find out where he does belong.

All good stories have a call to the world of adventure. YA is no different. There must be a problem that needs solving, a person who needs saving, some reason for the hero or heroine to step out of their ordinary world, stick their necks out and risk everything. The call can come in all shapes and sizes. Harry Potter received an amazing invitation to adventure if you think millions of invitations delivered by owl and magic qualify as an attention-grabbing call. However, he couldn't answer the call on the first invite, and there are many examples of even refusals from reluctant heroes.

2.   *Refusal of the Call*
Avoidance

The refusal of the call is an important part of the journey because it signals to the reader that the journey is risky. Pay attention. Trouble could be ahead. It also forces the hero to examine the adventure carefully and maybe redefine his or the journey's objectives.

Sometimes the call to adventure isn't really a call. The hero gets shoved unwillingly into the world of the adventure. In the first *Harry Potter* story, the refusal of the call isn't done by him. It's done by the Dursleys who are terrified of Harry becoming even more strange and different than he already is. Mrs. Dursley's sister was Harry's mother, and everyone knew she was strange. The Dursleys keep Harry's letters, which are invitations to Hogwarts, away from him, so he can't answer the call to adventure.

But even the most heroic heroes will sometimes hesitate or flatly refuse The Call. After all, a journey into the unknown can be downright terrifying. In the case of a hormonal teen hero, they may already be dealing with personal problems, emotional confusion and conflict. They are distracted. If they notice the call, they turn away from The Call as just another problem they don't want to deal with. Even if they're not in the most ideal place emotionally, the comfort of the familiar, of home, is a tough separation. The stiffer the refusal, the more the readers enjoy seeing it worn away.

Excuses

Heroes most commonly refuse The Call by starting a laundry list of weak excuses. It isn't their problem. there are many people more able to deal with the problem. They don't know what to do. They're scared. They will make the problem worse. Or, perhaps they don't view the problem as that important. In the case of a teenager, the most common will be that they're only a kid and how can they be expected to tackle such a problem by themselves? It should be left to the professionals, or at least to some adults.

Persistent Refusal Leads to Tragedy

Persistent refusal of the Call can be disastrous. Remember Lot's wife who denies God's call to leave her home? She looks back and turns to a pillar of salt. If the hero refuses the call enough, it can lead to a horrible consequence that forces them to pay attention, to enter the adventure, to journey forth before more tragedy strikes. It may even be revenge, but a reluctant hero must be given a motive to accept the call.

Willing Heroes

Some heroes are willing and even seek out the Call to Adventure. Other characters may express fear, warning the reader and the hero of what may happen on the road ahead. Luke Skywalker's uncle reminded him of his responsibilities at home. Harry Potter's uncle refused to let him go, trying to steal all Harry's invitations, even moving the family into hiding to prevent Harry from accepting the Call to Adventure. This is when a little outside help arrives.

Threshold Guardians

Heroes who overcome their doubts and fears concerning the call may be blocked by powerful characters who question and test the hero's worthiness. In *Harry Potter and the Sorcerer's Stone*, the Dursleys were the threshold guardians. Harry's first call comes when he receives a letter in the mail. Then floods of letters arrive, all fended off by the Dursleys as guardians. When owls start dropping off invitations to Hogwarts, the Dursleys are in a panic. If Harry leaves, who will clean their house and wait on them? And then he could end up like Mrs. Dursley's brother-in-law, a wizard! So how can the hero/heroine overcome such a powerful obstacle and cross the threshold to begin their journey?

Every hero, especially an inexperienced, frightened teen, needs a wise protective Mentor to guide, teach, train, test, provide magical gifts and prepare the hero for The Hero's Journey. There are many possible mentors to choose from. Luke Skywalker receives a lightsaber and advice on the force from Obi-Wan Kenobi. Harry Potter receives a magic wand on a shopping trip with Hagrid.

3.   *Meeting the Mentor/Supernatural Help*

Sources of Wisdom

Even if there is no actual character playing the Mentor, the hero must contact some source of wisdom before committing to the

Adventure. An ancient scroll, a prophecy, a solved puzzle, a map, an artifact or message left for them by a deceased or non-present entity will work. A teen could receive inspiration from a deceased parent via diary, letter, will, or video.

Mentors in Folklore and Myth

Heroes in mythology and folklore seek the advice and help of witches, wizards, doctors, spirits and their gods. These translate beautifully into modern-day urban fantasy or science fiction creatures. Harry Potter is teaming with fantastical creatures, acting as messengers, protectors and familiars.

Chiron: A Prototype

The centaur Chiron was the prototype for all Wise Old Men and Women. He mentored many of the Greek heroes. So, a human, a creature, or a cross between the two is a perfectly acceptable mentor.

Mentor Himself

The term *mentor* comes from the loyal friend of Odysseus named Mentor. In YA stories the mentor is often a friend. Hermione is always giving Harry advice or aid. Often friends help the hero/heroine keep from making mistakes, or taking unnecessary risks, although they can also challenge and motivate them.

Avoiding Mentor Clichés

Keep your writing fresh and avoid stereotype. You can still utilize the powerful custom of archetypes. They are the foundation for all hero's journeys.

Misdirection

The mask of the mentor can be used to trick the hero. Use the reader's expectations and assumptions to surprise them. A faithful friend can turn out to be an enemy, a shifter, or the hero/heroine can have a reason to doubt them and then discover they were their friend all along. Doubt is a powerful emotion and a very useful plot manipulator. The reader will want to find out what is going to happen.

Mentor/Hero Conflicts

Sometimes a mentor can turn villain or betray the hero. An overprotective Mentor can lead to a tragic situation. The mentor can be so controlling, trying to force the hero/heroine not to take chances or risk danger that they get in the way of the hero/heroine's progress and become a trial on their journey, an obstacle that must be overcome. Often such a situation results in death of someone important, even the mentor.

Mentor-Driven Stories

Sometimes an entire story can be built around a mentor. For Example, *Goodbye, Mr. Chips.* The rather strict and unyielding school master runs a very severe classroom until he meets and marries a delightful woman, Katherine. She so changes his views and demeanor he becomes an endeared instructor, loved and respected by everyone, as is his mentor, Katherine. The mentor can be as compelling and interesting as the main character. The mentor may also have been in the hero's shoes, so are in their own rights a hero.

Mentor as Evolved Hero

Mentors can be regarded as heroes who have become experienced enough to teach others. Many once held the position the new, younger version hero now holds, so they have already gleaned all the experience and knowledge the hero needs. Some examples include: Dumbledore from the *Harry Potter* series, Gandalf from *The Lord of the Rings*, Obi-Wan Kenobi from *Star Wars*, Merlin from King Arthur and the Knights of the Round Table, or Alfred from *Batman*. All strong, fascinating characters in their own rights.

Critical Influence

The mentor's brief appearance is critical to get the hero past the stage of doubt and fear. Mentors are extremely useful to storytellers. That's why we see so many of them and such a variety. They help move the plot forward, head the hero in the right direction down the right path in the journey. They help them avoid or overcome obstacles, warn them of danger, and even sometimes protect them.

Harry's first mentor, and one who sticks with him through all the books, is Hagrid, a kindly giant with a massive beard and a big heart. Hagrid knew Harry's parents and can tell Harry about them and how he's famous in their world. Harry learns there are Muggles and he thinks the Dursleys are the biggest Muggles of all. It's Hagrid's job as a mentor to show Harry his new world. The Weasleys also figure as mentors because they help Harry find his way to the mysterious departure gate.

4.   *Crossing the First Threshold*

Your hero and heroine are on the threshold of their great adventure. They are about to step out of their Ordinary World and into the Special World of their journey. There's more than one way to accomplish this as a writer. Here are the most effective.

Approaching the Threshold

There are several ways and scenarios you can develop to shove your hero or heroine across the threshold. Maybe a villain forces them across. You can also develop your story so that your hero runs out of options. Some heroes get shanghaied into their adventures this way.

Threshold Guardians

The threshold guardian is a powerful and useful archetype. They can pop up and block your hero's way at any time. They create obstacles, test and trials that must be overcome to step across the threshold. Harry had no knowledge of how to get on the train, how to find the station number. When he asks a conductor on the platform, he becomes even more confused. The secret entrance is an obstacle, itself a threshold guardian. The Dursleys were also threshold guardians for Harry Potter's first adventure. They kept him ignorant of his past and his heritage.

The Crossing

This crossing is a big moment in your story. Countless movies illustrate the crossing with actual physical barriers – doors, gates, bridges, deserts, canyons, walls. In *The Fugitive*, Harrison Ford leaps off a damn and into the Special World of being free. It's common for film editors to shift into Act II by changing the energy – sometimes using music or a drastic visual contrast. The pace of the story may pick up.

The actual crossing may be a single moment or a long passage. It's up to you and your story. To make this jump, your hero will have to muster an extraordinary amount of courage. This leap is irrevocable. Your hero can't turn back. Like Tris in *Divergent*, once she jumps on the train, there's no going back. For Harry, once he walks through the wall and onto the train platform nine and three-quarters, there's no going back.

Rough Landing

Heroes don't always enter their Adventure easily. They may literally crash into the Special World. According to a metaphor used by Disney – a story is like a plane flight. Act I is fueling, loading, taxiing and heading down the runway toward take off. The first threshold occurs the minute the wheels leave the ground.

Harry crosses the first threshold into the world of adventure in a very literal way. He has to find platform nine and three-quarters, and when he can't, he gets help from the Weasleys. He literally passes from the world of his normal life, into the world of his adventure. It's a beautiful moment in the book and for Harry.

5.   *Belly of the Whale*

Vogler eliminates this step from Campbell's pattern analysis and several others that are spiritual or metaphoric in nature as opposed to specific plot steps. It's understandable, as it simplifies the pattern; however, in a YA novel this can be a very essential story element, especially if you are working with a coming of age theme. Most writers have heard of Jonah in the belly of the whale, but you may not understand the allegorical significance of this in a coming of age novel.

Entering the belly, which symbolizes the womb image, signifies rebirth, a separation from life, as in dying to be reborn. The hero is swallowed up by the threshold. Compare is to the vacuum suck of swirling disorientation of entering a Stargate. The hero, like Alice, shrinks and plummets down the rabbit's hole, steps through a wrinkle in time, or is teleported to an unknown existence. The hero is lost, disoriented and confused and must regain his/her footing and equilibrium, being reborn after a complete transformation. This is fitting to a YA story, as the hero/heroine is about to undertake an inward journey as well as have an outward, literal adventure. It is essential that the YA writer remembers to nurture and develop this internal transformation.

INITIATION

6.   *The Road of Trials*

The hero/heroine must undergo a series of trials in order to begin their transformation. Let's face it, the plot is all about conflict, conflict, conflict. The hero may fail some of these tests or trials, and they often occur in threes. Each can become progressively harder with the hero learning even from failures to become more equipped to successfully complete a trial.

Vogler calls this portion of the hero's journey Tests, Allies and Enemies, because the hero/heroine goes through many trials, or tests, and makes friends and enemies along their way as they strive to overcome the trials set before them. Enemies are often there to test the hero, and friends often have special gifts to help the hero succeed.

While your hero is getting used to the Special World, there will be lots of tests. This is the most important function of getting used to the Special World and preparing for the big challenge or trial ahead. These tests are like Pop Quizzes meant to sharpen the hero, so he can pass the finals. Many mentors follow their heroes into this stage of the journey. Hagrid, Dumbledore and Harry's two friends, Ron and Hermione, stay with Harry through all the stories.

Harry's first challenging test at Hogwarts is the Sorting Hat. He and his two friends are all put in the same house, Gryffindor, but not until a rather confusing struggle to figure out why he could be in either Slytherin or Gryffindor and Harry himself chooses to answer the call and enter the world of Gryffindor.

The school itself provides Harry with challenging experiences. He meets ghosts, finds trolls in the bathrooms, three-headed dogs in the basement, and magic mirrors that will swallow your soul. He has two good weapons in his wand and his cloak of invisibility, but they can't help him win a brutal Quidditch match. For that he needs heart, tenacity, determination and bravery, things a hero must develop and possess in order to succeed.

Allies and Enemies

Allies and Enemies are essential in YA fiction. The tests Harry faces in *Harry Potter and The Sorcerer's Stone* are not as complicated or as deadly as the troubles he encounters in later books, but Harry finds Hogwarts's has its dangers and Voldemort is ever lurking in the background. Meeting new people, learning who he is and how to adapt to a completely different world all provide challenges. This is where Harry will learn the skills he needs to make it through the rest of the books.

In this section of the journey Harry not only gains knowledge important to his growth as a magician in the Special World of Hogwarts, but he also makes important allies who last for the rest of the series of stories. He also starts to collect enemies. His two permanent buddies show up immediately, on the train. Ron Weasley and Hermione Granger support, mentor and help Harry through all the books.

By this time the reader has learned Voldemort is Harry's enemy. He killed Harry's parents and left the scar on his forehead as a constant reminder. The lightning-bolt scar warns Harry by hurting whenever Voldemort is near.

Harry quickly identifies Draco Malfoy, and Draco's crummy little toadies, Crabbe and Goyle, as his enemies. They're like the boys back in the Muggle world who bullied him. This Slytherin trio is opposed by the Gryffindor trio of Harry and his new allies Ron and Hermione.

Harry also makes Allies and Enemies of the teaching staff. Hagrid who is a mentor is also an ally of Harry's. Professor McGonagall, who was a cat when Dumbledore dropped Harry on the Dursley's doorsteps, is also an alley. She provides Harry with a broomstick for the quidditch match. His ultimate ally amongst the teaching staff is Dumbledore who is always a faithful mentor as well.

Enemies also abound among the staff. Snape, is an archetypal Trickster. You never know if he is really a bad guy or a good guy, and Quirrell is in cahoots with Voldemort.

There are several kinds of allies and enemies in this section of the journey.

Sidekicks

This is an ally who rides with the hero through the Special World. The sidekick supports the hero. There are many famous sidekicks throughout literature. Sherlock Holmes had Dr. Watson. Frodo and Sam, Batman had Robin. Ron and Hermione often fulfill this function. Sometimes the sidekick can provide comic relief as well as assistance.

Teams

The testing stage sometimes provides the opportunity to forge a team. In romances, the testing stage is a good time for the hero and heroine to share experiences and forge bonds. Ron, Harry and Hermione form this kind of team during this stage of Harry's journey.

The Rival

This is a special type of enemy, the hero or heroine's competition in love, sports, business or anything at all. The point is that they are competing for the same thing, even if it's just to be better at it, like being a better wizard. The rival is usually not out to kill the hero, just defeat them. Malfoy is this kind of enemy.

7. The Meeting of the Goddess

Campbell includes this step to explain the receiving of gifts from a higher being. Call it kismet, divine providence, an eternal truth, luck, or the cosmos, the hero always receives something to help them at the critical climax. Harry received a wand, a cape, a map (in the Prisoner of Azkaban), information, and many other items to help him with his quest. King Arthur received a sword. Alice received an elixir. Perseus received a flying horse named Pegasus, a shield, a sword, and immortality. Always remember to provide your hero/heroine with special gifts to help them overcome their seemingly impossible obstacles.

8. Temptation

Yes, you can think Eve in the garden, or Delilah or any significant character that might lead the hero/heroine astray. This is a very controversial portion of Campbell's steps, since he was discussing ancient and medieval myths and texts most feminists consider misogynistic. Historically women have been very maligned here, so feel free to have males represent temptation. Woman here is used as a metaphor for any physical or material temptation in life.

Don't limit yourself to people. Think temptation. The hero/heroine is tempted to give up their quest, to care more for something or someone more than the greater good. They are distracted, and their quest slowed at the very least. To complete their journey, they must put aside all temptations to move beyond themselves. But let's be honest. Teenagers are easily tempted/distracted by love interests. It's a great plot twist.

9. Atonement with the Father

The hero must now confront whatever holds power over their life. According to Campbell, this is often a father figure who holds sway over their very life. Although this enemy confrontation is often pictured as male, it doesn't need to be male, but rather a very powerful, aggressive force. Harry confronts Voldemort. He must atone for the harm he has caused to others in his quest to confront Voldemort but must also seek justice. In an almost Oedipus complex way, the hero wants to kill the villain, hates him, and yet feels guilty for his hatred, fears becoming the very monster he fights and struggles with the inevitable need for survival. Harry Potter certainly does all this in his battle against Voldemort.

In a female version, Alice confronts a Queen, of hearts, no less. She must atone for entering the rabbit hole, but most also seek justice. The use of this internal character struggle adds an incredible depth to your hero/heroine that will suck your readers in and have them turning pages as fast as their eyes can take in the words.

Vogler combines steps 7, 8 and 9 into a step he chose to call approach to the Inmost Cave. We will further clarify steps 7–9 with more modern examples and clarification. Having made the adjustment to the Special World, the hero goes off to seek its heart. On the way they find a mysterious zone with its own threshold guardians, agendas and tests. This is the approach to their target, the Inmost Cave.

The function of the approach is to ready the hero for the final Supreme Trial. As the hero gets deeper and deeper into the Special World they may discover a need to make plans, do some reconnaissance, reorganize, thin out their number of supportes, fortify and arm themselves before going over the top into No-man's Land. This is the function of the Approach which has several rules and opportunities along with its own threshold.

Courtship

A romance can develop at this stage, bonding the hero and the heroine before they face the main ordeal, adding higher stakes, the desire to keep another safe at great risk to themselves, and also provides another ally.

The Bold Approach

Some heroes boldly stride up to the castle door and demand to be let in. Confident, committed heroes will take this approach. Or your hero may just be ignorant of the danger behind the door or in the city as he boldly rides into the Inmost Cave, the belly of the whale.

Preparation for the Trial

This may be a time for further preparation, rearming, checking of weapons for the trial ahead, or getting some indication from a mentor of what's ahead.

Obstacles

Having made some allies and some enemies during the testing stage, the hero faces a series of challenges and obstacles that will strengthen his resolve, bond him to any teammates and prepare him for the life-and-death struggle yet to come.

Beware of Illusions

This message is clear: don't be seduced by illusions, stay alert. What the hero think is true may be a lie and who he/she trusts may not be on the hero's side. It could be a trap, another test.

Threshold Guardians

Often the way to the Inmost Cave will be blocked by a threshold guardian. Past experiences from the testing stage and other stages of the journey will provide the hero with the skills and information he needs to pass this guardian. In *Harry Potter and The Sorcerer's Stone*, meet Fluffy.

Another Special World

On the other side of the Approach the hero will find another Special World. This world could have new rules and new values. It can be even more deadly, and the hero's trusty weapons have no effect in this new world. The hero will quickly need to adapt, learn new ways to cope with his/her new problems and develop even more skills. Think of when Harry went to the world quidditch match. It was yet another world, with harsher conditions and dangers, although at first the illusion was a place of wonder and excitement.

Be Prepared

The hero will know he's preparing for a great ordeal. Like a warrior sharpening his weapons, the hero must prepare for the ordeal ahead. It may just be mental preparation, where he thinks through the possible dangers and decide how best to deal with them, or a personal pep talk to gear up for what's to come.

Warning

It is good for your hero to face his trial balanced and prepared. But he needs to be warned. Often a mentor or an enemy will deliver this warning. Harry is warned by Professor McGonagall not to go after the stone because it is too well protected. Of course, that doesn't stop him, but he knows the danger.

Another Threshold

Often the hero will have to pass through several layers or thresholds, plot twists, to increase the tension. When delayed by more obstacles, the hero has a better chance to get to know his team members and the heroine. This is where, after getting past Fluffy, Ron and Hermione help Harry get through the three tests.

Emotional Appeal to a Guardian

Sometimes when experience is not enough to get the hero past the gate, an emotional appeal will work. The guardian will see the hero's sincerity and pure motivation and feel he/she deserves to be allowed across the threshold.

An Impossible Test

This impossible test could be the hero's need to face inner demons before he can face the main ordeal ahead. The hero may have to face this crisis alone because the people who he naturally turns to when in trouble will push him away.

Complications

Heroes may have disheartening setbacks at this stage. Such reversals of fortune are common and may be a good pace setter for a sagging middle. Although they seem to tear the hero apart, they just further test his willingness to proceed.

Higher Stakes

Another function of the Approach stage is to up the stakes. The reader may need to be reminded of a "ticking clock" or "time bomb." This may include adding such a plot device. Everyone, including the hero/heroine knows what the goal is, but maybe it's time to escalate the hero's motivation, his desperate need to achieve that goal.

Reorganization

The approach stage is the time to reorganize, promote some team members, sort out the living from the dead, tend the wounded and assign special missions.

Heavy Defenses

Heroes can expect the villain's castle to be heavily defended. If they don't have a difficult obstacle to overcome, what is the point of all the preparation?

Who is the Hero at this Point?

The Approach is a good time to recalibrate the team, express misgivings, give encouragement and determine that the right people are in the right job. Anyone who has doubts may challenge the leader and/or encourage him/her to give up, or even refuse to go any further themselves. Your hero's response to these circumstances tells the reader a lot about who the hero is at this stage.

Get into Your Opponent's Mind

Here the hero may put on a disguise to conceal his real intentions as he gets closer to the Inmost Cave. The hero may employ the device of "getting into the skin" of the threshold guardians. Harry has his father's cloak given to him by Dumbledore to get him through the final ordeal.

No Exit

No matter how hard your hero tries to escape his fate, sooner or later all exits will be closed off and the life-or-death issue must be faced. He's in the belly of the whale and must remain there until he has learned his lesson, accomplished his task, received the boon.

When Harry, Ron and Hermione arrive in the room on the 3rd Floor, Fluffy, an extremely large three-headed dog apparently loyal to Hagrid, is guarding the trap door leading to the Philosopher's Stone which Harry wishes to save from Professor Snape. Fluffy is asleep, and a magical harp is playing music.

This is Harry's approach to the Inmost Cave. He must pass this and perform the series of three tests (like the three days in the belly of the whale) to reach the next stage, which is the Supreme Ordeal. As they are trying to move one of Fluffy's paws and open the trapdoor, the enchanted music stops and Fluffy wakes up. They are forced to jump down the trapdoor as Fluffy tries to attack them. Any fear that they had about going on to find the Philosopher's Stone is now futile. There is no way back. They must go forward. Each of the trio takes the lead in one test.

Hermione uses her spell and herbology knowledge to rescue them from the Devil's Snare. Harry puts his seeker skills to good use to find the flying key with the broken wing to open the door. Ron leads the game of Wizard's chess to get them through this obstacle. Ron falls at this obstacle, and Harry leaves Hermione to look after Ron as he descends to the Inmost Cave to confront Snape and The Supreme Ordeal. Only it's not Snape, it's Quirrell. It helps to have good buddies along, but when the hero enters the deepest cave, he/she must do so alone.

10.   Apotheosis

Quite simply, this is the crisis, the highest point of tension, the "oh no, he/she is not going to make it" moment. This is the point where Harry is attacked, and it looks as if he's going to die. The clock strikes midnight and Cinderella races down the steps and out of her glass slipper. Katniss struggles to survive the finals of the Hunger Games. This is also the point of the story where a greater understanding is gained by the hero/heroine. Vogler calls this step The Ordeal, and it is. Only through this step can the hero/heroine achieve peace and fulfillment.

Now the hero stands in the deepest chamber of the Inmost Cave, facing the greatest challenge and the most fearsome opponent yet. This is the heart of the matter. The Ordeal itself stands separate from the other trials Harry faces, and you can tell right away that it's more serious than his other tests. Earlier, Harry and his friends have the teachers to bail them out. And while no one wants to see Malfoy make that smug little grin, at least they're not in any real danger of being killed.

That all changes once they get past Fluffy. There's no Dumbledore here to pick them up when they fall. Even worse, they're headed straight to Voldemort—or at least the incarnation of Voldemort living behind Professor Quirrell's head like a malevolent boil. Failure here is, in Dumbledore's words, "a most unpleasant death."

Harry ends up losing Ron and Hermione before the ordeal is over. Not permanently, but they get sidelined before the big dance with Voldemort. Harry must face the final ordeal on his own. In his Ordeal, Harry is tested both physically with the fire and the wrath of Voldemort, and morally when Voldemort tells him he can bring Harry's loved ones back to life. Harry emerges with flying colors and Voldemort is banished to the land of see you in the next book.

Death and Rebirth

The simple secret of the Ordeal: heroes must die before they can be reborn. The dramatic moment readers enjoy more than any other is death and rebirth. It is here they confront their greatest fear. It is at this moment they are transformed and rebirth occurs. Their resurrection rewards them with greater powers or insight, internally, and often externally as well.

Change

Heroes don't just visit death and come home. They return changed. It's the hanged man in tarot, his viewpoint turned upside down. Different perceptions and enlightenment, these are characteristics of a resurrected hero/heroine.

The Crisis, Not the Climax

The crisis or the Ordeal should not be confused with the Climax of the story. The Ordeal is usually the central event of the story or the main event of the second act. The hero meets the greatest trial yet, and often comes out the winner, but not without great cost. He/she emerges stronger, more prepared to journey forward and meet whatever greater trials await.

Placement of the Ordeal

The most common pattern is for the death-and-rebirth moment to come near the middle of the story. This leaves plenty of time for elaborate consequences to flow from the Ordeal.

Points of Tension

A story that has no central point of tension will sag (sagging middle). This is so important we will discuss this issue in its own chapter.

Witness to Sacrifice

The reality of a death-and-rebirth crisis may depend upon Point of View. A witness is often necessary, someone standing nearby who sees the hero *appear* to die, often literally.

A Taste of Death

Adventure films and stories are popular because they offer a less risky way to experience death and rebirth, through heroes we can identify with, or through the eyes of those we don't care emulate, like anti-heroes.

The Elasticity of Motion

Good structure works by alternately lowering and raising the hero's fortunes, and with them the reader's emotions. This is the roller coaster effect. Keep the tension high, then give the reader a breather. Think of it like music. There is a reason they use dramatic music to help set the mood in movies. Staccato notes depict a thundering heartbeat, fear, excitement, or physical exertion. In words, this translates to short, even choppy sentences where only the action or emotional upheaval is revealed. Neither a reader nor a movie-goer can keep this pace up indefinitely. That's why after the crescendo, the tempo evens out, slows down, perhaps not completely, but enough to let the reader/viewer relax and look forward to the next big event.

Hero Appears to Die

When the hero appears to die, the reader gets the ultimate emotional drop. Conversely when he lives again, emotions ride higher for having been sent so far down.

Hero Witnesses Death

When the hero witnesses the death of someone close, like a mentor, he will feel it as keenly as his own and be changed. The reader too will be affected. There are 76 deaths in the *Harry Potter* series. What reader wasn't affected when Dobby dies? Harry is devasted, and so were we.

Hero Causes Death

The hero doesn't have to die for the moment of death to have its effect. The hero may have to kill someone as part of his Ordeal. His innocence dies. He is changed forever. Harry took the deaths very seriously. He felt responsible and did his best to try to save everyone, even risking his own life to do so. The reader is right there with him, wishing him well, rooting for him, feeling devasted when he fails and jubilant when he succeeds.

Facing the Shadow

By far the most common kind of Ordeal is some sort of battle or confrontation with an opposing force. It could be a deadly enemy, villain or even a force of nature. It could be a Death Eater, or it could be a game of Quidditch.

Demonization

Generally, the Shadow represents the hero's fears and unlikable qualities, all the things he doesn't like about himself and tries to project onto other people. This kind of projection is called Demonizing. Harry gets so angry, he wants to kill Voldemort, but because he's a hero he realizes that will only turn him into a murdered. He would have to lower himself to Voldemort's level, and become a shadow himself.

Death of a Villain

Sometimes, during the Ordeal, the hero comes close to death, but it is the villain who dies. But the hero may have other forces and Shadows to deal with before the adventure is over.

The Villain Escapes

The villain that escapes will need to be confronted again. So, Voldemort is temporarily vanquished, but will return again.

Villains are Heroes of Their Own Stories

Many villains don't think of themselves as evil at all. In their own minds they are right. It's a good exercise to walk through your story in the villain's skin.

How Heroes Cheat Death

Many have come to this point (The Ordeal but none have survived. The hero is expected to die, but he beats the odds and lives.

Ariadne's Thread

Ariadne's thread is a potent symbol of the almost telepathic link between people in love. It is an elastic band that connects the hero with the ones he loves. This tie can pull the hero back from the brink of death.

Crisis of the Heart

The Ordeal can be a crisis of the heart. It might be the moment of greatest intimacy, something all persons desire yet fear. This can be either a love scene or a separation from a loved one.

Sacred Marriage

During the Ordeal, the hero may be forced to balance the opposing forces within his soul, bringing about a mystic marriage, a balancing of the inner and outer forces.

Facing the Greatest Fear

For most people this is death, it's just whatever the hero is most afraid of.

Standing up to a Parent

This can be your hero's greatest fear as well and can be a common theme in Young Adult and Middle Grade fiction.

Youth Versus Age

This may be a battle between child and parent such as Romeo and Juliet.

Death of the Ego

In myths, the ordeal signifies the death of the ego. This is a pivotal moment, especially for a YA. Most teens are discovering who they are. Death of Ego causes them to realize some of their previous beliefs are wrong, and they need to rethink their goals or motivations. They realize how some of their choices may have been based on misconceptions or wrong information. They begin to reconsider their path and choices. Where do they go from here? How can they gain the strength to move forward? This is an inner death of their past, a maturation and spiritual enlightenment.

11.   *The Ultimate Boon/Reward*

The hero realizes the magnitude of what he has experienced. He is overwhelmed and although triumphant, he needs to take a big breath, almost like the letdown after achieving all you ever wanted. What now? The transformation has occurred. He is no longer the person he was when he began his journey. How does he feel about it? How will he deal with it? "We came, we saw, we kicked its ass." *Ghostbusters*

With the ordeal behind him, our hero experiences the results of surviving.

Harry wakes up in the hospital after his ordeal and must wait for his Reward at the End of Term banquet. Gryffindor are transformed from fourth place for the Hogwarts Cup into first place by the extra points that Dumbledore awards for Ron, Hermione's and Harry's actions in stopping Voldemort gaining the Philosopher's Stone. With Voldemort gone, the Philosopher's Stone is safe from his clutches and he has to stay in evil smog form until he can figure out some other way of bringing himself back to life, and Quirrell quite literally blows away in a stiff breeze.

Celebration

This is the first thing your hero will do.

Campfire Scene

In Dances with Wolves, Dunbar is sitting around the fire with his Indian friends telling and retelling the story of saving the boy from the buffalo. In these scenes the audience catches their breath while the characters reflect. We grow closer to the characters through shared intimacy. This is an excellent time for a love scene.

Seizing the Sword

This is where the hero actively takes possession of whatever it is he's been seeking in the Special World.

Elixir Theft

The Theft of the Elixir may intoxicate the hero for a brief time. But there is always a heavy price to pay.

Initiation and New Perceptions

After an ordeal the hero often emerges as special or different. He may find himself with new powers or better perception of life.

Seeing Through Deception

A hero may be granted new insight or understanding of a mystery as a Reward. He may see through deception if he has been dealing with a shapeshifting partner. Seizing the Sword can be a moment of clarity.

Self-Realization

After the Trial, the hero might see himself clearly for the first time.

RETURN

12.   *Refusal of the Return*

Why go back to the ordinary, mundane existence the hero had before? He is not the same person and is no longer satisfied with his ordinary life. Harry had no desire whatsoever to return to the cupboard under the stairs after his magical experiences at Hogwarts, and who could blame him? Having obtained bliss and enlightenment, the hero may not want to return, even if it's to bestow the boon on mankind.

13.   *The Magic Flight*

Sometimes the hero/heroine must escape before he/she can return. This leads to a whole new set of adventures.

14.   *Rescue from Without*

Just as the heroine needed guides to help her achieve her goal, she may need powerful guides to help her return to her everyday life, especially if she is injured or weakened, which she quite easily might be, by the ordeals of her quest.

15.   *The Crossing of the Return Threshold*

This may be trickier than it seems. The hero needs to retain all he has learned and integrate his newfound wisdom into his everyday life. He may also need to share his wisdom with others. Poor Harry. He obviously matures and has learned to keep his own temper in check, against all odds, but his family seems incapable of learning must of anything outside the reach of their own noses.

16. **Master of Two Worlds**

Harry Potter learned to negotiate Hogwarts and become a wizard and he also, through his trials and tests, acquired the ability to be tolerant, patient, and better deal with his admittedly impossible family.

17. **Freedom to Live**

Mastery leads to freedom from death and thus the freedom to live. Harry no longer fears his own shadow or the admonition of his family. He can maintain his servitude with the knowledge that it is only temporary, and the Dursleys, no matter how much they might wish to, can't prevent him from returning to Hogwarts or from becoming a powerful wizard.

Creating and

Peopling

Your Y A World

Chapter Four

Creating a Real Young Adult World with Real Teens

When you talk about world-building, many writers think you're talking about fantasy lands like Narnia, Westeros, Panam or Middle Earth. For most teens, school is their world. What kind of home life they have is their world and these worlds need to be just as complicated as Narnia. Well-developed teen worlds like Hogwarts, North Shore High School, home of the Mean Girls, Rydell High School of Grease, and Panem of Hunger Games are so well-developed they seem real, and you remember them as though they were a place you visited.

To create a real world for teens in our times, you really need to know them: what they do every day, what they like, what motivates them, the environment in high schools and many other details. Home life for kids is very different from twenty or even ten years ago. It takes two incomes now to support a growing family or to succeed, so both parents most likely work. This leaves kids as young as nine or ten at home alone for long periods of time (or even younger, unfortunately). The enemy of these parents is the school holiday, and it seem like there's more than ever. These parents have no idea what to do with their children. Many can't afford childcare, so the kids are home alone. It's a thing you must think about when writing for them.

Children come from all levels of society. Poor kids will view the world through different eyes than kids who have well-off parents. Kids living with a single parent might have a different view of the world as well as different social structures. The kids with single parents or working parents might have to go hungry on weekends, on school holidays and especially during the summer. It's hard to think about, but true. There are teenagers out there who eat breakfast and lunch at school and their families provide dinner. Sometimes all they get is their school meals some days. When school is out, they scavenge and fend for themselves or they don't eat.

Grandparents must step in and take care of kids due to the opioid crisis, families self-destructing, working parents and teenage pregnancies. Some of these situations lead to older children taking care of younger siblings. This matures some teenagers rapidly. They lose out on childhood. It makes a great theme for young adult fiction. Living with grandparents can change these children's lives. They go from no supervision to strict supervision, or sometimes from strict supervision to weak or inadequate supervision. There's another theme, too, open rebellion because of the beliefs and morals of an older parental figure.

These modern-day themes and problems sometimes can be translated to other times and other worlds. Some things never change.

Romeo and Juliet arrive in the twenty-first century. Poverty and hunger in the sixteenth century or in a dystopic future. The way teens react to situations is often repeated generationally. Some kids step up and become heroes and some melt down and need help from peers and mentors.

Every parent of a fifteen-year-old girl knows this one. Teenagers dealing with the pressure of school, the social scene and family life exhibit mood swings because of stress or just because they're teenagers. They often have no reason you, as a parent, can discern. A teen's emotions can run the gamut from ecstatic to sad, complete with corresponding actions, including rude comments, foul language, shouting, slamming doors and crying for no "apparent" reason.

Rebelliousness

When teenagers begin to assert their independence from parents, they might engage in rebellious behavior. It's a universal attribute that gets them in trouble and can help you, as a writer, invent great stories. Like Tris in Divergent, "no more boring Abnegation. Give me Dauntless." The sixties were the time for lots of teen rebelliousness. None of them wanted to go to Vietnam. There were marches, signs and the times changed.

Teenagers are full of hormones. Guys have too much testosterone that can fuel anger and rebellious behavior. Girls have hormones too, which can lead to sneaking out at night, or rebelling in other ways. Teen pregnancies can result from hormones, rebelliousness and two working parents—or present nonexistent parents.

Perfectionism

Among teenagers, perfectionists are real and most often populate the Popular group, the jocks, and the cheerleaders. These kids are terrified that if they let one thing slip, no one will like them anymore. Their hair, their clothes, their teeth, their school work, all must be perfect. Not only does this class of teen strive to impress their perfection on their peers, but many have a genuine fear of not being loved by their parents if they aren't perfect.

Whether they're hoping to impress others or simply imposing high standards on themselves, teens struggling with perfectionism can end up with permanent problems because perfection is impossible to maintain. It takes these kids a long time to learn they can be loved for themselves and they don't have to impress anyone. Some may go through their entire lives and never learn this.

<u>Need for Approval</u>

Everyone needs approval. Teens can be especially needy. It's a time in their lives when they're possibly suffering from self-confidence issues. They need ego bolstering to get through each day. Maybe there's no parent at home to give it or maybe their parents don't have the time. Teachers and administration officials must function as surrogate parents all the time, but especially for this group.

This neediness could be the catalyst that pushes a teen into proving something to a peer, something they aren't normally inclined to do, something outside their comfort zone. This can end with them doing drugs, getting drunk or experimenting with sex. Girls are often more susceptible than boys. Having a boyfriend bolster a flagging self-image with compliments can make a teenage girl feel on top of the world. This is where the most impressionable fall in love and then must deal with repercussions that can be life altering; pregnancy, breakups, public attention. Even though girls are more susceptible, boys can be needy as well. They might not want humiliation from rejection.

The needy kids are the ones who require the means to fit into a peer group and do things they know are wrong to feel accepted. This need to fit in can lead to risky behavior, smoking, drugs, drinking, driving too fast. Keep this in mind when writing for kids. Think about *Grease*. Sandy wanted to fit in. Did she make the right choices?

So, you know your characters and you want to create a world where they can exist. How do you do it?

Scope

First you need to figure out the scope of your book. Is it huge? Are you fighting battles in outer space? Do you need a galaxy or two? Or are you writing a contemporary book about kids in a small town going to a small-town school with a football team, cheerleaders and bullies? That's the scope. Once you've got how big or small you want to make your world figured out, then you put flesh on the bones of the world you're constructing.

Rules

Every world you create, whether it's a fantasy world, a world in an apocalyptic future or a small town in middle America, needs rules. For example, if you're writing about vampires, what kind of vampires are they? What kills them? What doesn't kill them? Is holy water deadly or does it just roll off their skin? Can they fly? All these details fall under the heading of rules. You lay out the rules and keep track of them, because vampires that can't fly in chapter two, can't suddenly fly in chapter nine.

If, in your dystopian future, there is no water and your characters are dying of thirst. You must figure out a way to provide them with water. Maybe one character falls through a hole in the crusty desert and lands in a spring. Water, yay. If you create a character that is allergic to shrimp and he eats shrimp in chapter six, he better get sick. These are rules you lay out and must follow throughout your book. Sometimes these rules can cause problems. If your character needs to kill a vampire and only has holy water and in the beginning of your book you said holy water did nothing, then you better think fast. Your character better think fast and come up with a way to kill this vampire "within" the rules you created.

Society

Inside your book you need to create a society. This could be the students in the school, the faculty, the cliques and the bullies like *Grease* or *Ferris Bueller's Day Off*. Your characters interact with these members of the society. Your school needs walls and floors. They need to be institutional green or blue or gray, and the floors highly-polished or worn-out wood or faded linoleum. The desks and computers might be brand new and shiny or old and scarred. Does the average classroom have twenty or forty kids? Details make this world real.

If you're writing about an apocalyptic future, it needs to be peopled, or maybe not peopled as in they all died. Are there zombies like *Zombieland*, or groups of marauders and scavengers like *Book of Eli*? Are there towns filled with survivors who have created a working society based on pig poop like *Mad Max Beyond Thunderdome*? Is it a city like Mos Eisley in *Star Wars* where different aliens roam the streets? If the scope is larger, maybe your character lives in a distinctive community like District 12 in *The Hunger Games*. What you create will be the society of your world.

Inside your society, whether it's real or fantastic, the people, human, vampire or extraterrestrial will have certain commonalities. They will share certain elements and infrastructure.

1.   **Language.** Everyone in your world needs to be able to understand each other. Or maybe they don't and some of your characters speak different dialects, so they will have to work out a common language.

2.   **Sports and Recreation**. For example, Quidditch in the *Harry Potter* stories or racing and working on hot rods in *Grease*.

3.   **Politics or Hierarchy**. This could be as simple as the hierarchy inside of a school clique or as huge and complicated as the government of Panam in *The Hunger Games* with its rules, president and the annual Reaping. Hogwarts had political issues and an administrative hierarchy.

4.   **Beliefs.** This doesn't have to be religion. It could be a belief in magic like in *The Craft*, belief in the rebellion in *Star Wars* or the belief in the factions in *Divergent*, even though this belief was being challenged by the Divergents. These core beliefs generated action and conflict.

5.   **Values.** Some of these values might be morals that tie into the belief system. People in Panam allowed the government to take two of their kids every year and potentially kill them. They believed it was morally acceptable until the Mockingjay showed them it wasn't. The rebels in *Star Wars* believed the morals of the government in power were corrupted by the dark side of the force, while they were fighting for the good side of the force. A basic good against evil. Values can also be tangible like money. Does your world have a barter system or run off regular money? In *Guardians of the Galaxy*, units are used as a form of currency. In *Waterworld*, fresh water and dirt were valuable in the barter system.

6.   **Taboos.** Each world will have things that are off limits. The maze was taboo to everyone but the runners in *The Maze Runner*. In *Divergent*, if you left your faction at the choosing, it was taboo to talk to your family or anyone from your past life in the faction you left. In *The Hunger Games* you weren't allowed to leave your district.

7.   **Commonalities.** This includes shared enemies, shared experiences, a shared heritage, shared tragedy and a shared climate and environment. All the Reds in the *Red Queen* knew if they didn't have a job or an apprenticeship, they were going to be conscripted and sent off to fight the war. In *Harry Potter and the Sorcerer's Stone*, all

the kids and teachers except one, were afraid of Voldemort. The kids all lived at the school and shared their experiences and environment.

8.   **Atmosphere.** Atmosphere is the mood, the feeling, the tone of your book. If it's a book set in an apocalyptic world like *Book of Eli*, make it feel apocalyptic. *Book of Eli*, *The Maze Runner*, *Mad Max Beyond Thunderdome* and the most recent *Mad Max: Fury Road*, really feel like they're in an apocalyptic world. It's the atmosphere. In the last film of *The Lord of the Rings* trilogy, *The Return of the King*, the atmosphere made Frodo's journey even more frightening. If you're writing comedy, strive for lighter atmosphere. Think *The Game Plan*, *The Hot Chick*, *Matilda or Diary of a Wimpy Kid*. And then there's horror. Young adult books go there. *Twilight*, *City of Bones* and *Miss Peregrine's Home for Peculiar Children* all had horror elements and a dark, brooding atmosphere.

Things to Avoid When World Building

<u>Ignoring Basic Infrastructure</u>

If you choose to write about either a dystopian society or a science fiction or fantasy world you must think about the basics. How do they eat? What do they eat? Who takes away the garbage? Who deals with their bodily wastes? How do they get around? What do most people do to survive? You're not just constructing a society, you're creating an economy.

Maybe you need a lot of peasants to grow labor-intensive crops, or maybe you need lots of cannon fodder in your space war. Maybe your only source of protein is a weird fungus that needs to be tended by specially trained people. Maybe everybody's eating worms or bugs. In any case, there's nothing worse than a fictional world where there are elaborate social structures, which seem completely separated from the realities of food, shelter and clothing. In *The Hunger Games*, the world of Panem, every district had a job. In *Divergent*, every faction provided something to the survival of those living in that world.

Leaving the Reader Ignorant of the Causative Event

Like *The Hunger Games or Divergent*, if the world you're creating revolves around an apocalyptic event, the readers need to know what it was. *Divergent* didn't address this until much later in the book, or completely until book two, *Insurgent*. Why is there a Reaping? What happened to the world seventy-five years ago to make this the seventy-fourth Hunger Games? These questions must be answered. You can't just start off in a world that's living off grubs and mealworms and not explain how that came about. In *Harry Potter and the Sorcerer's Stone,* you knew in the first chapter why Harry had to live with the Dursleys. If you open your book with three kids stuck in the bottom of a well, the reader will want to know how and why that happened.

Don't Forget to Give Your World a Strong Sense of Place

You can spend hours developing infrastructure and a society that is totally unique, concentrate on setting and getting your characters dressed according to where they live, the time and location, whether it's in a fantasy land or Des Moines, and completely fail at creating a real, believable world. If you don't make the reader feel the dirt of your character's dust bowl farm under their fingernails or smell the stench of the garbage in the inner-city alley behind their homeless shelter, then you still haven't created a real place.

Even on Tatooine, in Mos Eisley, there was a bar with recognizable booths and music. No matter how weird the world you create, there must be a few places where your reader feels comfortable and at home. If it's a high school, the gym or a classroom that's recognizable. The world of *Weird Science* began in the gym. You knew the kids were real before they made a woman with their computer because they were in the gym being bullied. All the crazy stuff that happened after was grounded in Wyatt's room, and that high school gym where it ended, a place where the viewer felt comfortable. In *Guardians of the Galaxy*, Star Lord had a fast-paced start that dumped him in a city square with something very familiar in the middle, a fountain. Grut got a drink when Rocket appeared. A weird character doing something very normal. You must make your world vivid and alive, but also provide something the readers can relate to, something comfortable.

Details

So, once you have the world and its rules clear in your mind, your job as a writer becomes making it as real in your readers' mind as it is in yours. Details can flesh out your world. They can be selectively used to highlight tone and atmosphere and used to add humor, sensuality or suspense. Enter vampires who sparkle. Thank you, *Twilight*. Try as we might, we can't get that image out of our heads.

Chapter Five

Archetypes Add Character

Archetypal characters appear in all religions, mythologies and epics of the world, making them universal. They resonate on a subconscious level to everyone, like an innate knowledge of good versus evil.

Hero/Heroine

First, no matter what, you must have a hero/heroine. A hero is most often the character willing to be selfless, to give up, however reluctantly, his or her own needs for the good of others. Joseph Campbell calls *archetypes* an expression of our personal and collective unconscious. All archetypal heroes/heroines share certain characteristics. Following are five major ones.

- **Courage** ~Courage and bravery leap to mind first when we think of heroism. Despite the reluctance with which the hero may accept the call, the point is that the hero does. That person often puts him or herself at great risk for the greater good.

- **Selflessness** ~Few teenagers are saints, and if the hero was a saint, she wouldn't be very interesting either. Heroes may be selfless as a side effect of being impulsive, even reckless, with that immortality viewpoint many teens have, which leads to their thrill-seeking extreme sports enthusiasm. Nevertheless, even if they have pressing problems to deal with, they don't turn away from the bigger picture, the most important world-changing problem that needs to be addressed, putting their own problems on the back burner if need be.

- **Humility** ~Only an anti-hero sports a heavy dose of hubris. The hero acts from a need to do what's right, to help someone in need, to change the world for the better. They aren't looking for pay or accolades, although they may not turn them down if they're offered.

- **Patience** ~Tenacity might be a better word to use when speaking of a hero/heroine. Heroes don't give up at the first trial or obstacle. They keep forward-focused and get the job done.

- **Caring** ~Even if they say they don't care (we're talking teens here), the hero/heroine's actions clearly show that they do.

The Anti-Hero

The defiantly reluctant ones are known as anti-heroes. They don't want to be heroes, are thrust into the role by accident, by a friend or by a need. Think Tyrion Lancaster if Game of Thrones. This character isn't always the main hero and may be a reluctant side-kick to the hero, but the reader loves to see the interaction between them.

Anti-heroes have become very popular. Ever watch *Breaking Bad* or *The Sopranos*? What about *Dexter*? The anti-hero is the protagonist who lacks traditional hero qualities. He or she isn't selfless, kind or noble. The anti-hero lacks moral goodness and is riddled with flaws and demons and angsts. Anti-heroes march to the tune of their own agenda.

They aren't a villain, per se. There is something so compelling, so sympathetic about them, that we are truly rooting for them to win, to beat out the traditional "good" guys. How many perfectly sane people didn't want Dexter, a serial killer, to get away with murder?

There are varying degrees of "lacking" in these anti-heroes, and there is always some dark backstory to make them seem sympathetic and to help the reader understand why they are as they are. They may very well save the world, but they believe they should get paid for it. There needs to be something in it for them. The important thing about an anti-hero in a story is that the solution isn't possible without that character, whether the anti-hero is the main hero or not. Without that character, a story with an anti-hero in it has no story. So, if you want to use an anti-hero, make sure you use them correctly. Think about the *The Dark Knight*, or *Maleficent*, Heathcliff from *Wuthering Heights*, or any number of main characters from *A Game of Thrones*. Anti-heroes are interesting and unpredictable and as much fun to write as they are to read.

Readers love anti-heroes because they're flawed and they're fascinating. This is the age of the anti-hero. They make us feel better about our own mistakes and encouraged to find success wherever our starting point may be. This is especially enticing to teens, who are still spending a lot of time learning from one mistake after another. They love to read about flawed, struggling characters who help them realize not everyone has to be perfect or fearless to have value. It makes their own flawed lives feel suddenly more worthwhile. Being human rather than super human is not only relatable, it's appealing.

Sometimes these anti-heroes violate everything we've been taught to expect from a hero, including the need to play by the rules, follow the law, or help old ladies cross the street. They're the bad boys or girls that parents have warned you about, making them even more appealing because of their obvious undesirability. Kids live in a world filled with violence and extreme selfishness, witness public corruption and crazy celebrity meltdowns. They know no one is perfect. They're not perfect and they want to read about flawed heroes with mixed morals and world views.

Like a hero, the anti-hero is strong, tenacious, and with single-minded focus will pursue his goals. That's often why that character stretches the borders of accepted social morals and bends a few laws. But one heroic thing even an anti-hero must have is a pure motive. When characters do bad things for good reasons, they're anti-heroes. Today's YA readers love anti-heroes.

Mentors

Every hero needs some help, and teenaged heroes need them more than an adult might. They get their help from mentors. Mentors listen to them, instruct them, and most importantly they understand them. That's because an archetypal mentor has been in the hero's position. Hagrid was once a student at Hogwarts. In *The Hunger Games*, Haymitch was a tribute. The mentor often seems a bit "off." This character is disheveled and rumpled and harried or distracted. The character gives the reader the impression that the hero is doomed to failure if the hero must depend upon the mentor's help to succeed. The mentor is a bit of a misfit, and live alone, although everyone knows and likes him or her well enough. Sound a lot like Hagrid? Often, mentors are known to drink a bit too much, too. But the hero needs help and advice. Mentors, no matter their flaws, provide it.

Once the hero either consciously or unconsciously chooses to start on his journey, his guide or magical mentor will become known to him/her. Like Hagrid, this mentor will be bigger than life and will present the hero with talismans or artifacts that will aid him later in his quest. Hagrid gives Harry the first money he's ever had and takes Harry shopping where he buys his wand, a magical tool he will use throughout all his adventures.

Allies

No teen wants to go anywhere alone. Teenage girls don't even like to go to the bathroom alone. They need allies. Even loners like Kelly Leak in *The Bad News Bears* ended up joining the team. YA fiction and movies always involves teams. Kids need friends and allies to get through life, so your young adult book needs a variety of allies to support your hero. Samwise was a wonderful ally to Frodo in *The Lord of the Rings.* Katniss had Peeta and Gale, and Harry had Ron and Hermione.

Herald

The herald is an odd archetype. He or she, or even it, often appears only long enough to announce the need for change in the hero's life. The herald is the catalyst that sets the whole adventure in motion. While the herald character often bring news of a threat in a distant land, he can also simply show a dissatisfied hero a tempting glimpse of a new life. Occasionally he singles the hero out, picking the hero for a journey he wouldn't otherwise take.

Effie in *The Hunger Games* was the announcer at the Reaping. She held the role of Herald briefly before she became a mentor. She's the one who called Katniss' sister's name, drawing Katniss into the adventure when she took Prim's place. R2-D2 was a herald carrying the message from Princess Leia. He continued into the story where he became a companion for Luke. In the classic fairytale *Cinderella,* the herald was Cinderella's invitation to the ball.

In *The Maze Runner*, the boys received a letter heralding the arrival of Teresa. In *Divergent*, Four plays the part of the herald when he explains that not all Dauntless initiates will be allowed to enter the faction. In *Jumanji: Welcome to the Jungle,* the herald is literally the herald driving the Land Rover who arrives as they land in the game and explains the rules. Heralds don't need to be human, either. In *Harry Potter and the Sorcerer's Stone*, an owl plays the role of herald.

Trickster

The trickster is a fun and very important archetype, often introduced to cut some of the tension and add humor to a dire situation. The trickster lands in the middle of the mundane and shakes things up. Dobby and Fred and George Weasley played the roles of trickster in the *Harry Potter stories*. A darker trickster is the Joker in the *Suicide Squad*. You never knew what he was going to do. He popped in and out of the movie, keeping everyone jumping. Merry and Pippin from *The Lord of the Rings* provided many lighter moments in a scary world of adventure. The Cheshire Cat in *Alice in Wonderland* was a trickster too.

Shapeshifter

The shapeshifter archetype blurs the lines between allies and enemies. The shapeshifter can start out as an ally, then at a critical moment, turn on the hero and become an enemy, making a dire situation seem hopeless. In YA fiction, shapeshifters fill your typical teenagers' desire to be able to turn themselves into someone else, change their looks on command, and go from nerd to popular kid.

The more traditional role of a shapeshifter is to bring up the question of loyalty. Shapeshifters are two-faced or maybe two-natured as werewolves are sometimes called. As they waver back and forth with their loyalty, they provide a tantalizing combination of appeal and possible danger. Gollum in *The Lord of the Rings* is this kind of shapeshifter. In *Star Wars*, when Darth Vader changes his loyalty to his son, Luke, he becomes a shapeshifter. This kind of shapeshifter can benefit your stories by creating interesting relationships among the characters, and by adding tension to scenes filled with allies.

In *Harry Potter and the Sorcerer's Stone*, the students take a class on shapeshifting called Transfiguration. Who wouldn't want to study transfiguration instead of algebra? On the first day of class, Professor McGonagall transforms her desk into a pig. In *Twilight*, Edward sparkles in the sunlight, captivating Bella, and sparks one of the biggest audience debates of all time.

Werewolves and humans who can change into other animals are also called shapeshifters. This is one of the most common themes in fantasy literature whether it's young adult or written for adults. The idea that you can change into someone else or become a beautiful animal at will is captivating. Bella eventually gets turned into a vampire. Jacob, the other boy competing for Bella's affections, is a werewolf. In *Alice and Wonderland*, one pill makes you larger and one makes you small. Teenagers love shapeshifters. Although a werewolf changes shape, that monster might just be a monster who changes shape. The role of the shapeshifter might be to confuse or delay the protagonist – making the reader wonder if the shapeshifter character is friend or foe.

Threshold Guardian

The threshold guardian archetype is usually a character created to keep the hero from passing through the threshold into the world of adventure. However, the threshold guardian can appear at any stage of the story. It's the threshold guardian's job to test the hero before she faces great challenges. The message to the hero is clear: don't go, forget it, stay home.

The Dursleys as threshold guardians want Harry to stay home and forget Hogwarts. In *The Fellowship of the Ring* the threshold guardians arrive in the form of the Black Riders as they make several attempts to prevent Frodo from passing into the world of his adventure. They also have a message for the reader, this way is dangerous. The Dursleys did their best to keep Harry from going to Hogwarts. In *Divergent*, Tris's parents try to convince her she should join their faction, Abnegation.

There are several guardians in *Jumanji: Welcome to the Jungle* as there are in the *Harry Potter* series. In *Jumanji: Welcome to the Jungle*, there are threshold guardians to every level. Bikers appear when they try to reach the city. In the city, they must pass the snake. When they need an aircraft to fly them to the jaguar mountain, there are two guards in front of the hanger. Each threshold guardian presents the group with a test that is passed by different members of the team. In the first Harry Potter book, when Harry needs to find the Philosopher's Stone, Harry, Hermione and Ron must get past the guardian of the trap door, the three-headed dog, Fluffy, and then perform three tests requiring a skill only possessed by one of the team.

Threshold guardians provide an important element of your book. They make the quest harder, add tension and suspense and plot twists. Always throw everything you can at your heroes. When the going gets tough, make it horrific. Nothing worth having comes easily.

The Shadow

Shadows are your bad guys, the villain. Create a good one because villains are sometimes the most complex and interesting characters in your book. In *The Hunger Games*, President Snow smells bad. He has a disease that causes him to smell like death, which adds to his creep factor. In the movies, using Donald Sutherland to play Snow was a perfect choice. His dramatic pauses and powerful image add to the aura of evil and danger surrounding him.

Darth Vader is another great bad guy who also ends up as a shapeshifter. Voldemort is so terrifying no one will even say his name. Having him murder Harry Potter's parents before the story even starts adds to his mysterious presence and his fear-factor. Miss Trunchbold in *Matilda* will always be one of our favorite villains. She was the headmistress from hell. Every kid loved to hate her.

Shadows might be governments or aliens. In *The 5th Wave*, Colonel Vosch was the visible arm of a horrible alien invasion. He wasn't the real villain. The real villains remained in the shadows. Darth Vader was the emissary for a much greater evil, the dark side of the force. The emperor was another emissary for the real evil. The dark side of the force mirrored the good side. The battle for Luke's soul was a great way to show the conflict between good and evil. This is a common theme in many YA books. The battle for good against evil. Miss Honey in *Matilda* against Miss Trunchbold, for example. *The Lord of the Rings* is the ultimate good versus evil series. The good wizard Gandalf had to face two evil wizards, the evil Sauron and Saruman.

It's important to give as much care to creating your villain as you do your hero. Villains are complex and need a full backstory, or they will appear as mere cookie-cutter figures and won't create the fear and emanate the aura of danger you need to write captivating YA fiction.

Characters can represent more than one archetype in your work. Effie in *The Hunger Games* wasn't just a herald, she was also a mentor.

Any character that represents more than one archetype is more important to your story. Just as you need to cut words, you need to cut characters who don't serve an important purpose in your book. If they don't represent at least one traditional archetype they should probably be cut.

Chapter Six

Characters are How You Keep Modern Kids Reading Your Books

Creating believable and interesting characters is the most important thing, and the best fun you can have writing YA fiction. Making your characters real, making them different, making them appeal to teens is crucial to the success of your work. You need to understand teens are very social but are still learning to socialize. This leads to angst, stress, and emotional freak-outs any parent can relate to. Why is my kid losing his/her mind? The answer is often their friends or lack of friends.

Modern teens have a wide variety of friends. They tend to divide themselves into peer groups or cliques, which is something you must understand to write for them. They are trying to figure out who they are, so they identify with various traits they see in others. These cliques of kids who share various characteristics are formed and reformed over the years, but many remain on a friendly basis, no matter what direction their interests take them. Teens live and breathe through their friends, and their friends are usually like them in a variety of ways.

The story that best portrayed these varied groups is *Jumanji*. In the recent movie, *Jumanji: -Welcome to the Jungle* (based on the book series by Chris Van Allsburg), the lead character was a video gamer, self-proclaimed nerd. The team contained a jock, a "mean girl" type, and a geeky girl. When they entered the game, they changed into game characters. This transformation as they entered their world of adventure changed their opinions of each other, and those they used to look down on. They took those changed opinions back into their real world as their reward. It's always wonderful when your characters grow. In fact, in YA Fiction, it's essential.

Another YA series that portrayed teens' tendency to join cliques is *The Maze Runner* by James Dashner. The characters living in the world of the maze gravitated to certain groups that could be considered equal to modern high school cliques. These groups performed certain tasks that made living in the glade possible. Thomas, the lead character wants to be a Runner. There are also Slicers, Sloppers, Baggers, Med-Jacks and Builders. Runners were top of the list. The boys with this most important job were mapping the maze. They had to be fast, smart and risk-takers.

Divergent by Veronica Roth is all about being in a clique or group. When the protagonist rebels and leaves her parents' boring faction, Abnegation, for a younger, wilder faction, Dauntless, it's like a modern teen going from being a nerd to becoming a cool kid.

The groups teens form in high school will also differ according to location. High school in Hawaii isn't going to have the same cliques or groups as a high school in Salt Lake City, Chicago or Portland. This must be considered when writing. In St. Augustine, the cliques in the school closest to the beach are different from the schools further out in the country. Same county, same district, but different kinds of kids attend so the cliques will be different. This can also be different in schools with kids from different socioeconomic backgrounds, and private schools. Keep your setting in mind when developing your character's traits and friends, and vice versa. Be sure they are believable and seem accurate, even if they're all made up.

Basic Teen Social Cliques

1.   **Jocks and Cheerleaders** These types of teens have been working to attain this elevated position most of their lives, sometimes pushed by mothers and fathers who are trying to live out their own lost dreams through their kids. *Varsity Blues* shows this parental shoving clearly as the lead character's father rejoices when his son's high school football team's, the Coyotes, quarterback is severely injured, and his son gets the job. You can see it in *Remember the Titans* as parents try to push their own bigotry onto the kids of a high school football team.

Jocks are athletes. This teen category has been around forever. You can spot them by their t-shirts, school colors, varsity jackets and letters, and running shoes. They're the teens who live for their chosen sport, which could be basketball, golf, weightlifting, wrestling or any other high school sport. This category isn't just for boys anymore -- many girls are jocks as well. Adults often tend to look on these students as leaders among their peers, and instruct them on responsibility, self-discipline, teamwork, and competitive excellence.

Football players are at the top of the teen hierarchy and for this reason are tricky characters. Most teens don't fit into that niche, and teenagers want to read about kids that are like themselves. According to teens who were interviewed, the students most likely to turn into bullies come from this group. However, teens who participate in sports often do better in school than the ones that don't. Athletic departments provide their athletes with tutoring, and other additional help to make sure they keep their grades high enough for eligibility mandates. They get scholarships, they're driven, and they often go to college.

Cheerleaders are often the pretty, athletic girls. They wear makeup, trendy clothes and frequently come from affluent families. They like to date jocks, can be sexually active and often become a group many young teens call "mean girls."

2.   **Popular Kids** These kids can be Trendies, Jocks, Cheerleaders or even Geeks or Nerds. They have personalities that naturally draw others to them. This can also be another source group for bullies. They have a following of either other popular kids or kids wishing they could be popular. Outcasts from the Middle School categories sometimes drift into high school and keep hanging onto the desire to be one of the popular kids, but eventually they get smart and realize it's not going to work and fall into some other category.

The movie *Mean Girls*, starring Lindsay Lohan as a girl negotiating the jungles of teenage subcultures, put a new label on this type of teen who is often one of the Popular girls. In this movie, the group was known as the Plastics. They wore high heels, short skirts, or whatever the latest fashion was. They formed exclusive cliques and gossip was their native language. They picked on everyone they felt was their social or physical inferior and that was almost the entire school. Mean girls crave popularity, and it's often explained as being because they feel insecure. Being plastic, they have a hard time with genuine relationships. They cultivate "frenemies," which are girls they hang with but secretly hate. Even their BFFs (best friends forever) might be spurned tomorrow. These mean popular girls who fall into this category make great shadow/villain archetypes. They're the girls all other girls love to hate.

3.   **Geeks** are obsessed with something. It might be computers or computer games, comic books, anime, Star Wars or superheroes. It may even be a school subject or activity. There are math geeks, science geeks, and drama geeks. They are usually your intellectual group, and very, very good at whatever it is that holds their obsessive attention. They could be socially awkward and possibly make odd fashion choices, or they could have lifelong friends used to their inattentiveness as they over-obsessive about something that fascinates them. They usually do well in school, but maybe only in subjects that grab their interest. They fall into the Science-Fiction, Fantasy-lover category and could be the biggest readers in high school, which would make them one of your more important target audiences.

4.   **Nerds** are like geeks but smarter. They might have been called brains or teacher's pets growing up. They're the first kids with their hands up, and they always have the right answer. They might not have the fashion sense of other groups, and they usually prefer chess to basketball or football. At one time, anyone who understood the mysteries of computers was considered a nerd. Now, a whole generation is computer savvy, so modern nerds might be the ones who understand the science behind the techno glitz or be impressive hackers.

Nerds may have emotional issues and or mental handicaps like OCD, eating disorders, extreme lack of self-confidence or learning, personality or emotional disorders like ADD, ADHD, PTSD, hyperactivity or they could come from broken and dysfunctional families. These kids are at risk for suicide and susceptible to social pressures to use drugs or try risky behavior to fit in. They may perceive themselves as unattractive and unlovable. They either hang out together or can be loners or even group with the Outcasts. They often consider themselves as different. They make great characters. They're conflicted, have unresolved issues, and they also could be huge readers.

5.   **Trendies.** These kids are dedicated followers of fashion and designer everything. They wear whatever is hot right now, probably too tight. They have strange hairstyles. Guys will be into gel and using lots of "product." Girls might dye their hair purple or add extensions, braids or any other style they think will get attention. Snapchat, Instagram and other forms of social media are essential. They will never be seen without a phone. Trendies, sometimes called scenesters, might get labeled *posers* or *wannabes*. There's a danger of some of them being drawn into drug and alcohol use associated with a club or scene, but not all do. One category of these Trendies goes in for the scene but rejects these dangerous trappings -- they're known as straight-edge scenesters. Trendies could also fit into the Popular category, the Jock category, but probably not the Nerd or the Geek categories.

6.   **Outcasts** are kids who don't feel like they fit into any of the categories. This may be a choice, because they can see through the phoniness of the cliques, or it could be forced on them because they're different. They are often kids from broken homes, most are introverts and loners who have grouped together for moral support. Outcasts or fringe kids from middle school can end up in this group when they discover the bad news that they won't ever be accepted by the popular kids. Some of these kids may eventually find a group they fit into. Some are genuine loners. They are one of the groups most likely to be bullied, but they can also have some unresolved anger issues and be very dangerous. These kids may be a good audience. They read. And they make great characters.

7.   **7.Skaters, Surfers and Snowboarders** are a diverse group of kids. They are usually physically fit. They hang together. Many are

attractive. They wear clothing that sets them apart. Their pants are baggy to give them room to maneuver, their shoes are oversized, have thick padded backs and heels to provide support and protect. They often wear oversized shirts. This style was copied by snowboarders even in their cold-weather suits. They have long hair. Girls wear the same stuff. They live for skateboarding, or in mountainous regions. for snowboarding. In cities and towns on coasts with surf, the surfers join this group. A skater might not be able to surf, but surfers are always also skaters. They can be more rebellious and are risk-takers. They would make an interesting hero or heroine.

8.   **Gay, Bisexual and Transgender** kids are more and more visible in high schools in this country. As the stigma attached to being sexually diverse fades, being in this group can even add drama and an odd popularity to members who are in this group or who claim to be. Some kids, usually girls, are unsure of their sexuality at this stage and may flit in and out of this group. Books including trans and gay kids are becoming not only acceptable but sought after. These kids could also be huge readers as they search for meaning, information about why they are who they are, and for literature that includes them. This category is growing larger every day.

All Out and *Meet Cute* are two trans YA books out in 2018 by Meredith Russo. *Let's Talk About Love* by Claire Kann, and *King Geordi the Great* by Gene Grant are gay offerings out in 2018. It's a wide-open market.

9.   **Rockers (sometimes called Head Bangers), Emos and Goths** are kids who wear dark clothes, may seem depressed, and as developed characters could easily demonstrate personality disorders such as bipolar disorder. **Emos** have roots in the punk culture. They want to appear rebellious. They have piercings, tattoos and bizarre hair colors. They're called Emos because they are highly emotional. **Rockers** are usually outcasts who stick together in groups with similar musical tastes. **Goths** rarely go out in the sun, highlight extremely pale

complexions, wear black make-up, black clothing, lots of jewelry, may have piercings and tattoos. They emulate characters from gothic horror movies such as vampires and make great YA characters. They can fall into the Outcast category as well and are possible readers.

10. **Gamers** play video games. This is an obsession with many. They could be into cosplay, and very into one certain game. This could be *Madden* (football) or a war game or *Minecraft, World of Warcraft, Call of Duty* or a science fiction game. Gamers can be introverted, but they may not be. Some play games with a team of buddies and run or belong to an online guild of self-formed team players. They live in the world of their games and may even ingame role play. Stanley in *Jumanji: Welcome to the Jungle* is a gamer and a nerd. Gamers could be Geeks as well. They must be computer literate and smart to play. Some gamers have a hard time dealing with the real world, and most feel it just gets in the way of their gaming. They play in the middle of the night, for hours on end, and might miss a lot of school.

Be careful to do your research when creating a gaming character. Games like *World of Warcraft* (WOW) have players of all age groups, around the world. They even have movies and video trailers about the game characters and storyline, "professional" world-wide competitions, playoffs and conventions. One of the biggest in-game jokes about a bad player in WOW is that they should get off their mom or dad's account and go to bed. Some older players got hooked by going in game to in fact tell their kids to go to bed on the in-game chat, which– complete with voice chat these days–is the only way these kids communicate outside of phone texts, about the game.

Some players have played for years, and whenever there is a new, long-awaited "expansion," such as the August 2018 Battle for Azeroth in WOW, avid players are going to be squarely in front of a computer, probably weeks ahead of release, previewing the Beta version and helping the company iron out bugs. All the while they will be getting their guilds updated and ready to attack the new dungeons and raids, gleaning all the new in-game goodies as soon as the release goes live. They will be talking of little else and annoyed to be pulled away for anything. They could be reluctant heroes alright.

11.   **Band Dorks** have existed forever and will probably always exist. They play an instrument, tote it around with them, belong to the orchestra and the marching band. They hang around together, have busy schedules, usually don't follow fashion trends and may not consider themselves physically attractive and are not considered by most to be cool. They're usually smart and have good grades, after all they have learned the discipline required to play an instrument and attend regular practice sessions and events after school. These guys read as well so consider them good characters for any YA book.

There are, of course, exceptions to this, and these days some high schools have an amazing flag or drum team that will blow you away. Their marching bands or drumline battling warriors compete all over the country, even globally, and are seen marching in the Macy's Day Parade. Those kids don't think they're dorks at all. In fact, they can be some of the hippest kids in school. Positions on their teams are highly competitive. As a writer you get to decide what traits your characters have. Just remember to stay true to the setting, circumstances and story.

12.   **Bad Boys and Bad Girls** can exist in any of the previous categories, but most often are either loners, jocks or cheerleaders. Especially in urban settings, they can be straight-up gangsters or wannabes, gang members even in Jr. high. Those could be anti-heroes or bad guy shadows.

Every girl wants a bad boy, so he can be an anti-hero, or change and not be bad anymore. Han Solo was a bad boy type and Princess Leia fell for him. Bad girls are popular for the obvious reasons. They fit into the mean girl role easily, but can be misunderstood, abused at home, lonely girls searching for love. They make great characters, as a member of one of your teams, or even a heroine.

13. **Ethnicity is Huge in YA** It is predicted that white people will be in the minority by 2050, maybe sooner. Editors and agents are looking for books featuring teens of all different ethnicities. They want the Asian, African American, Latinos, Mayans, Columbians, Middle Eastern, American Indian and kids from India. In short, they want real kids.

Ethnicity adds flavor. Many races have cultures that affect their behavior. Do your research and find the odd, quirky characteristic your ethnic character can use for fun, and to affect the outcome of your story. And remember just because a kid is African American or Latino, doesn't mean he also doesn't fit in one of the other groups, because you know he does. There are African American kids in the band, Latino skaters, and Pilipino cheerleaders.

14. **Rednecks** are prolific in the South, out West, and in mountain or farm country (rural). They love hunting and fishing, could be the sons and daughters of farmers or ranchers, and may ride horses, Western saddles only. They belong to the FFA and the 4-H and could have absorbed racial bias from their families. They wear jeans and boots and plaid shirts just as you'd imagine. Kids in this group could fit into other groups. They might be jocks, or popular kids, or fit into the outcast category.

Some of the boys might rodeo. This makes them very attractive to girls because they are usually fit, and then there's the cowboy hat. They fit nicely into a cowboy-type YA. If you're going to write about horses and cowboys, do your research. It's a specific world and teens who are active in it and might want to read your book will know if you fake it.

15. **Inner City Kids** have different lifestyles, more external conflicts to deal with in their life, and different groups in school. Some

have never left their block in their entire lives. Gangs are a major problem in inner-city schools and not just in the cities you think like Chicago or Detroit or Los Angeles. Gangs exist in smaller cities as gangs move into them to make more money.

The racial percentages change in inner-city schools. The overwhelming number of kids are ethnic, either black, Asian or Latino with white kids sprinkled into the mix. They could deal with more multigenerational drug-related issues, have single parents or even be homeless. Inner-city kids are more likely to have trouble with drug use, violence, sexual activity, drinking and smoking even among middle school kids. This presents all kinds of opportunities for stories about struggle and survival in a harsh environment, but make sure you do your research because the make-up and nature of gangs is constantly evolving. There are now white gangs in inner cities as well as ethnic gangs. There are now gangs and high heroin use in the suburbs. Do your research.

Middle Grade has Different Cliques

Since middle school has kids just coming out of elementary school all the way through eighth grade, their social systems are not as well developed as the ones in high school. Kids in middle school are in a strange time of their life. They grow and change in middle school like no other period in their development. They enter middle school terrified sixth graders and leave as suave and sophisticated eighth graders, hoping to be ready for high school.

There are four basic groups in middle school:

1.   **Popular Kids** are usually good looking, probably play sports, are cheerleaders, have outgoing personalities and come from more affluent homes. They wear trendy clothes and have the most friends. Having lots of friends can help you survive middle school, which, as in

Diary of a Wimpy Kid, Middle School: The Worst Years of My Life and Jessica Darling's *It List,* can be tough.

2. **Fringe Kids** are the ones who hang onto the coattails of the popular kids. These kids shadow the popular kids to become popular. Middle school is all about learning where you fit in. These kids often mimic the actions of the popular kids, dress like them, laugh like them, make the same jokes, but they're just not there yet.

3. **Friendship Circles** form in middle school. These kids sometimes come from the same elementary school, may have similar interests such as music, sports or the same hobbies such as skating or playing video games. They form these circles for support as they navigate the scary hallways of middle school.

4. **Loners** are kids with emotional problems or kids who may have just moved in from another state or city. They haven't figured out where they fit in and may never do so. They could haunt the fringes, jealous of kids who do fit into a group or who have large circles of supporting friends but can't or won't figure out how to belong. They are different from fringe kids only because they are currently isolated by their newness, their need to evaluate their surroundings and the norms in their new surroundings. They may eventually join one of the subgroups, or choose to remain isolated, either by their own choice or the refusal of subgroups to accept them.

There are subgroups within these four groups usually linked together by similar likes and dislikes, or activities. Kids who participate in sports usually make friendships with their team members and other kids who play sports. Kids who play in the band or sing in the chorus may form another subgroup. And even in middle school there are nerds, geeks, emos and punks. Some kids may belong to more than one clique. A redneck can be a jock. A geek could be a trendy.

Inside each of these groups, there's a hierarchy. The only clique that doesn't follow this hierarchy is the Outcasts. They stick together, united against a cruel world. Survival is the name of the game.

The female groups work somewhat like this:

- **Queen** is the leader. She rules because she's either the prettiest or through charisma had developed the largest following. She will usually be from an affluent family and could be strong-willed and manipulative. She often falls into the mean girl category. This hierarchy will work in most groups, but is best in either a cheerleader, jock, popular, trendies or maybe band dork group.
- **Sidekick**. This is the queen's second in command. She always supports the Queen's opinions.
- **Floater**. This girl can't make up her mind or has many talents. She can be a liaison because she flits in and out of the other cliques, may have friends in all of them, and gathers info for the Queen.
- **Pleaser**. This poor girl desperately wants to be in the clique. If given the chance, she immediately adopts all the Queen and Sidekick's opinions, yet never gains their approval and is often treated with indifference by the entire clique.
- **Target**. This is another girl who wants to belong but is not a member of the clique. She hangs around and is regularly excluded and humiliated by the Queen and the other members.

Male groups also have a hierarchy.

- **Leader**. This kid is like the Queen except well-respected, usually by the whole school. He's probably tall, good looking, athletic, tough, from well-off parents and he always gets the girls.
- **Flunky**. This guy takes the role of the Pleaser. He does anything asked of him, but he also responds to any member. He can be a jerk and annoying. He probably wishes he could be the leader and takes his unhappiness out on others.

- **Thug**. This is the group's enforcer. He might be smart, but you'd never know. He enforces the will of the group by being a bully. He fits into the group but may have received abusive treatment as a child.

You can see evidence of this hierarchy in *Divergent* and *The Maze Runner*.

Laying the Foundation: Characters

Characters are the foundation of your story. They're the concrete pad you pour your plot and action on top of and into. Without great characters you don't have a story. You have a two-dimensional, flat house, no walls, no sides, no floors, and it certainly isn't going up. Real, three-dimensional characters can take your book to the stars.

Characteristics of Memorable Characters

1.   **Flaws and Strength.** Nobody, especially not teenagers, wants to read about perfect characters. Unless, of course, you're talking about Dwayne Johnson as Dr. Smolder Bravestone in *Jumanji: Welcome to the Jungle*. When he pulled up his list of powers and weaknesses, he didn't have any weaknesses, and he was a great character. He wasn't immortal, however, and did die before crashing back into the game. Giving your protagonist a weakness makes them more human, more relatable to your readers.

Katniss Everdeen in *The Hunger Games* was kind-hearted and rough around the edges. Her weaknesses proved to be strengths in the end. But her love for her sister was the foot in her back that shoved her into the world of adventure. Think about the movie *The Goonies*. Every member of the Goonies had some interesting flaw, which is why we loved them so much and cheered when they were successful against the horrible Fratellis. And then there's the best flawed character ever, Greg Heffley from *Diary of a Wimpy Kid*. We loved him; he's wimpy.

In *My BFF is an Alien,* the two lead characters are deeply flawed. One has a Major in the Marine Corps for a father and is extremely OCD. The other is a Latino with Tourette's syndrome. Writing characters with flaws can be so much fun. The characters drive the story with their flaws, their desire to be popular, along with the stressful experience of finding an alien. Have fun with your characters. Make them interesting.

2.   Three-dimensional. It's so easy to say "make your characters three dimensional," but what does that really mean? How do you do it? There are many techniques you can use to add that extra spark to your characters and give them unique qualities that will set them apart from the rest.

First, give them a sense of destiny or a deep belief. In *The Goonies*, Mikey totally believes in the myth of One-Eyed Willy. His belief in that myth makes the entire story happen. Poor Mikey has asthma and hauls his inhaler around, but that just makes him more loveable, and his dedication to his belief makes him a complete, three-dimensional character. In *Livia Lone* by Barry Eisler, two Thai sisters are sold into slavery by their parents. Livia's journey to find her sister after they are separated, makes her a heroic, three-dimensional character.

3.   Character Growth. Whoever your characters are, whatever they are, when the story ends, they need to have become better. They need to grow. Frodo and Samwise are completely transformed by their journey. When they go home, their lives will never be the same. They discovered courage and fortitude they never knew they had. Thomas and the other Gladers of *The Maze Runner* that survive the trip through the maze get to know the reason they were there. All of them had to reach deep inside themselves to find the courage to face the Grievers.

The five characters who went into the game in *Jumanji: Welcome to the Jungle*, came out more socially aware and more accepting of different kinds of people. They came home with an understanding of what it's like to be in someone else's shoes.

Often, the boon, the reward, is knowledge or emotional growth that makes them a better person, more able to deal with their everyday problems and the people back home. They contribute more and offer hope and now experience in problem-solving to their community, friends and family. They may even bring back something needed to solve a problem back home, literally.

4.   **Emotional Depth (care about them).** The best characters are the ones readers fanatically love or love to hate. Regina George, in *Mean Girls*, was a character you loved to hate. Leader of the Plastics, she was followed around by two toadies, her best friends, Karen and Gretchen, and had mastered the art of making other girls feel inferior.

Everyone loved Harry Potter. Rowling put him in a closet under the stairs, servant to his aunt and uncle, and bullied by his cousin. You felt something for him immediately. The feelings your characters make readers experience give them emotional depth. For your readers to have feelings for your characters, you must care about them first, and that emotion, that empathy, is what gives life to the teenagers you create.

As if being a teenager isn't hard enough, add torment by persons in a position of power and a teenager garners instant empathy from the reader. They feel the character's pain. When the character is long-suffering, even as they have anger and frustration at the injustice, the reader immediately begins to root for them and to harbor dislike and even hatred toward the perpetrators of that injustice.

Draco Malfoy was a terrible bully, and Harry always had to worry about what he would say or do, wishing he could avoid him. Readers loved to hate Draco, but he became more complex and interesting once readers saw how his hateful father treated him. It suddenly became clear why Draco was the way he was. Readers might still hate him, but they understood him and even felt sorry for him, to a point. After all, he made his own choices, no matter what his motivation.

5. **Motivations.** Why do your characters do what they do? To create real characters, they must have a backstory, a past that supplies them with the motivation they need to get through their journey. Katniss Everdeen loves her sister and mother. She takes care of them. She's a huntress. It's this love of her family that leads her to take her sister's place in the reaping, and it's her inner spirit combined with the skills she learned feeding her family in the wilds of District 12 that give her the motivation, the ability, and the drive to succeed.

Harry Potter was motivated by a desire to discover what happened to his parents, to escape the Dursleys, and discover his talents as a wizard. He never wanted to be a hero, go up against Voldemort or save anyone, let alone all wizards.

Give your character a reason, something from their past or a dream for the future, that motivates them to undertake their journey and succeed. Otherwise no one will believe their sincerity, especially when they originally resist.

In *Holes*, Stanley Yelnats would never have headed across the desert if he hadn't made a deep connection with Hector Zeroni. Stanley had a good heart. And his trip to find Zero is what led to them discovering the treasure and ending the Yelnats curse.

6. **Hopes/Dreams.** When Thomas was shot into the glade in *The Maze Runner*, he came equipped with a strong desire, whether planted or just this own nature, to get out of the glade, to find a path through the maze, to discover why they'd been put there. Thomas's goal in the three *Maze Runner* books where he's featured is to survive and defeat WICKED, but the goal of those who first experienced the flares and the disease was to discover a way to save humanity. The tests and trials were their answer. Thomas was supposed to be their

cure. Whether this was right or wrong, that was the goal of the entire series.

Frodo had the most obvious goal. Dropping the ring in fiery Mount Doom to save Middle Earth was the driving goal that kept him going throughout the series. In *Weird Science*, Wyatt and Gary had a dream, a dream of being popular, getting girlfriends, and not being bullied--a goal millions of teens can relate to. So, they created a beautiful woman. The teens in *Jumanji: Welcome to the Jungle* had a simple goal, survive and get out of Jumanji so they can go home.

All these goals and dreams drove the action of the stories the characters were in. Without those simple hopes, dreams, goals, there would have been no story. This is how you make your characters three-dimensional. You give them a burning need that carries the story.

7.   **Secrets (leads to conflict).** Secrets characters keep throughout the stories can affect the plot of your story, its outcome and most certainly the characters' love life. Edward couldn't tell Bella he was a vampire and Jacob couldn't tell Bella he was a werewolf. Until this was revealed, there could be no romance between Edward and Bella. The biggest secret-driven story of all was Clark Kent hiding he was really Superman. This affected every aspect of the stories around him. Matilda's secret power affected the kids in her school positively, helped Miss Honey, but kicked Miss Trunchbold's butt. Hector Zeroni kept the secret he stole the shoes that put Stanley Yelnats in the boy's camp digging holes. He wouldn't talk. He kept his secret throughout the entire book. When he revealed his secret, Stanley didn't care that Zero stole the shoes. Zero was still his friend and Stanley still rescued Zero. They find the treasure, and the Yelnats family curse is lifted.

All these secrets drove the stories and created inner conflicts and outer ones that made the stories more interesting. Secrets are just another way to make your characters real. Everyone has a secret.

8. **Revealing Character by Dialogue and Actions.** One of the most successful uses of language to tell who characters are and point out that they're different is the slang created by author James Dashner for the kids inside the Glade. New kids are *greenies,* poop is *klunk,* a friend or fellow glader is a *shank*. When you hear any of these terms, you know where they came from if you've read the books or watched the movie. Effie Trinket in *The Hunger Games* was always fluttering; her voice and style of speaking were clear and definitive. You always knew it was her speaking in the book without a tagline. This should be your goal as a writer. Make your characters' actions, style of speaking and mannerisms distinctive.

One of the best examples of this is when one character becomes another. Think *Freaky Friday* when Lindsey Lohan, playing Jamie Lee Curtis's daughter, switches bodies with her mother, you recognize them because of their actions and speech patterns. Another movie like that is *The Hot Chick*. Rob Schneider, a disgusting criminal, changes bodies with a mean girl. When the girl discovers herself in the body of a man, she's the same girl, same mannerisms, same actions. You know it's still her. Schneider does a great job of showing that.

One of the best new movies that shows how each character's mannerisms and speech patterns are their own no matter what is *Jumanji. Welcome to the Jungle.* When the popular girl, Bethany, morphs into the game as Professor Oberon (Jack Black, an obvious guy) you still know it's Bethany in there because of the way he talked. Black did a super job at showing this, talking like Bethany and acting like her. When she hunts for her phone, so she can post something on Instagram, you see Bethany doing it even though it's Black. The other three characters, the nerd, the jock and the dorky outcast girl, all keep their original characteristics even after they morph into different bodies. It's a great way to see how voice, actions and speech patterns, can define a character and make a character more realistic.

9.   Create Empathy for Characters. This sounds like it should be easy. All you must do is make your reader feel a connection to your character. Easy, right? No, it's not. Cookie-cutter, flat characters abound. If you want to sell your work, create a readership, you must create reader empathy on page one. If you don't, your book won't be a success—that is, should you find an editor.

There are many ways to do this. Some of these ways we've already described above. Give your character a flaw or flaws so you feel his/her pain. In *Save the Last Dance*, Julia Stiles plays a girl from a small, midwestern town moving to the Big Apple. She gets off the train to go to her father's small apartment and you can feel how lost and alone she is. Then she relives her mother's death in her memories, showing you why she must live in New York and why she feels responsible for her mother's death. She's filled with so much guilt, she doesn't care where she is or what happens to her. That first scene draws you in. You immediately feel her pain. It's the way you need to start your book, with something that draws your reader right in.

The first scene in *The Hunger Games* book, you see Katniss in the woods, using her bow to hunt food for her family. She's moving through her dystopian world, bartering in the market. Then she's with her sister singing a song to her. You feel an instant connection to Katniss and her world. This is so well-done. In *Red Queen*, in the first scenes, Mare is stealing something. The author, Victoria Aveyard, shows the crazy world she lives in. The fear of being sent to war pervades every moment of her and her friend's life. You make a connection to her. In *The Maze Runner,* Thomas is catapulted into the Glade on the lift. He's terrified and confused. You connect with him and want to see him discover who he is and why he's in the Glade. Use your opening pages to connect your readers to your characters with empathy. This technique will make your characters three-dimensional and breathe life into them and your story.

Before you start writing, you need to know everything you can about your character. Many successful writers build a character chart about each main character in their books. If you are writing a series, you will be very happy to have this writing "bible." It can be as detailed as you want, but there is some basic information you should know about your main characters to give them depth and real personality.

Creating a Character Chart

Physical Description

This is basic, but if you chart it, then halfway through your book your protagonist won't suddenly have green eyes instead of blue. A basic physical description of all your characters is important. If you're writing about an ethnic character, make sure you note any quirks, languages, or cultural differences.

In this section, note any speech or language issues. If the character is ethnic, maybe from India, what kind of speech patterns does he/she use? Does your character swear a lot, talk fast, have a squeaky or high voice or a deep voice? It's always good to give your protagonist some kind of nervous habit such as nail-biting, clenching fists, shoving her hands in her pockets, or maybe he is overly friendly, giggly. Traits like these make your characters more realistic. Just be very, very careful not to overuse them, or to use them exclusively to develop character. A character who brushes her hair out of her eyes too often makes the reader long to give her a bobby pin. Don't let it become an *irritating* habit.

Does your character have odd habits? Does he drink gallons of coffee, eat compulsively, or not eat at all? How well does she sleep? Maybe your protagonist can't sleep. Maybe she has terrible dreams. If so, why?

Background/Environment

How many siblings does your main character have? Do his/her parents work? What kind of home does the character live in and in what world? Is it inner city or Middle Earth, the suburbs or some deserted island? If you chart what your character's bedroom looks like, it will be there to refer to throughout the book. How much time did you spend in Bella's room? In Edward's? What did it tell you about them? Well, for one thing, Edward didn't have a bed. What did that tell the reader?

Maybe your protagonist is homeless or from a broken home. Maybe they spend fifty percent of their time with different parents who have different families. Chart it, even if you add to it as the character tells you about it throughout the story.

Religion could be important to your character's background. It could affect their behaviors, motivations or ideals, even who they choose as friends.

Do they own pets? Chart the pet's name so you don't accidentally change it halfway through your book. Is it his ever-present companion, like another character in the book? Does it interact well with others? Does the character talk to his pet, rely on the pet for comfort, protection, or friendship?

When you refer to your character's family life, make notes about her childhood. Was it happy or troubled? Did she have a mean grandma who babysat her? Note her earliest memory and her saddest. Details like this make your book more real. Even if you don't use every detail, it gives you a better insight into the character, which helps you reveal more about him/her to the readers--just not in a huge, sappy background dump that doesn't move the plot forward in some way.

Does your character have a soft heart or is he cold and unfeeling? Why? Is he terrified to speak in front of the class or outgoing and boisterous? Is your character generous or selfish or somewhere in between? If he was an only child, sharing might be an issue. Is your character empathic and sensitive to others' needs or self-absorbed?

Hobbies and interests

Is your protagonist a band dork or a world class drumline battle champion? Does he/she fit into one of the cliques? Maybe the protagonist loves sports, computers, books, or animals. Does he cook, sew, paint, sing, love games like chess or backgammon? Chart these things so you don't forget and start your book with your character glued to a game box and then forget the addiction halfway through the book.

Make sure you note what kinds of friends the protagonist has and if her friends like the same things she does. How did they become friends? What do they have in common? Maybe your protagonist's best friend lives next door. Your protagonist is a band dork and the neighbor is a jock, but they're still best friends. What clique they fit into is an important detail because it tells so much about your character's interests, feelings, emotions, dress and acceptance in school.

Is your character struggling with problems at home? Is he/she a sneaky drinker, pilfering mom or dad's booze or pills or pot late at night? Does your character smoke? Many of these habits can be attributed to the clique the character belongs to or wants to belong to, and even keeps the character from pursuing the life he or she secretly desires.

Hopes (goals/dreams)

All characters in your book should have a goal. This could be as simple as burning desire to be popular, or as complicated as the desire to save the world. If they live in an alternate reality, like a dystopian future, a fantasy world, or a historical time period, their goals should be appropriate to that world. It's also important whether your character achieves that goal. You need to keep it in mind while writing your book. Also think about whether achieving his/her goals will affect other characters. For example, if the protagonist's dream is to join the military, how will her parents feel about it? Could something happen to change the character's goal? Could he have an epiphany and realize that what he thought he wanted isn't what he wanted all along, or that his goal isn't all it was cracked up to be, or the cost to himself or others is too great? The tests and trials set for the character by gatekeepers or guardians could end up altering the path her journey takes.

Aside from one main goal, does your character have minor hopes and dreams? What is his or her greatest wish? Maybe she's growing her hair, maybe he's trying to build his physique, add muscles. Maybe your character just wants to lose weight.

Fears

When writing for young adults, this will be important. Most kids are afraid of something, some kids are afraid of everything. Kids going from middle school to high school are afraid of high school. They could lose sleep for a week anticipating that first day walking the halls of a huge school.

Aside from general fears like being afraid to speak in front of their peers or being bullied in the bathrooms or at lunch, some kids have phobias. This can be an interesting characteristic to add to your protagonist. Maybe in a *Little House on the Prairie* situation, your main character is terrified of large animals. Or maybe in modern day life, your character is a germaphobe. Quirks like this, or fears, add an aspect of reality and makes your work more interesting. Cookie-cutter characters are boring.

Conflict

Conflict makes stories interesting. Does your character have a running fight with another school friend or a mean girl? Maybe a sibling or an abusive stepparent? Or maybe the conflict is an inner one. He or she is constantly battling the desire to run away from home or a bad situation and must stay because of finances or loyalty. The fight to overcome his fear of bullies or eating in front of people could be an inner conflict.

The story's major conflict could depend on the world you create. If it's a fantasy, maybe there are dragons to fight. If your story takes place in a dystopian future, maybe surviving against groups of marauders is the major conflict. In *The Maze Runner*, the conflict was discovering a way through the maze and out of the Glade while fighting the Grievers. And this conflict in *The Maze Runner* was manufactured by adults (guardians) to test the characters.

Drive (motivation)

Drive can come from two places in a story. It can be the force inside your protagonist that drives them to cross the threshold into the world of adventure. Katniss Everdeen in *The Hunger Games* loved her sister so much, she took her place in the Reaping. Her love for her family was her driving emotion and motivation. She was also a strong girl, with a lot of skills and a burning desire to survive. But, it was her heart, her kindness that motivated her actions in the story. When she cried over Rue's death, put flowers all around her body and held up two fingers for District 11, she won over the entire country and became the Mockingjay.

Thomas, in *The Maze Runner*, was driven to find the secret of the maze and a way out of the Glade. He was the only kid there who saw there was an endgame, a purpose. His drive and motivation pushed the other Gladers to act. Without Thomas, his drive to get out, the Gladers would have stayed there forever. That's what Gally wanted.

He loved the life in the Glade. He had a position of authority. He tried to keep the kids in the Glade even in the face of changes that would destroy them all.

The other source of drive in a story is external. Something happens that forces the protagonist to act. This external drive moves the story just as the internal drive does. In *Divergent*, the Choosing forced Tris to make her decision. Her inner drive made her choose to leave Abnegation and join Dauntless. In *The Lord of the Rings*, Gandalf forces Bilbo to give Frodo the ring of power. Then Gandalf explains to Frodo, Sauron's power is growing, and the ring must be taken out of the Shire. This is the driving force that pushed Frodo into the adventure, an adventure that will test Frodo in every way. Samwise Gamgee, Frodo's loyal friend, is driven by his fierce loyalty and love for Frodo to accompany him on the journey.

Matters of the heart

Every book written for young adults should have some element of romance. Teenagers are constantly falling in and out of love. Their affections are easily engaged, and romances blossom in high school on a daily basis. Great conflict can be obtained if you have two main characters vying for the affections of the protagonist like Peeta and Gale in *The Hunger Games*, and Edward and Jacob in *Twilight*. The conflict adds a lot of depth to the storyline. In *Twilight*, it is the story line.

Most YA has some element of romance. In *The Maze Runner*, there's Teresa and Thomas, in *Red Queen,* Mare and Cal Calore even though she's affianced to Cal's brother Maven and in *The Lord of the Rings*, which is not really a YA series but a series that appeals to everyone, there are multiple romances. Teens are interested in the mystery of romance so make sure you include a dash of love in your YA book.

Belief Systems

Belief systems don't need to be based on a specific religion, although they can be. Characters are sometimes abused in the name or religion, and then have issues with any religion. It can also be something they accept, having been raised to believe it as truth. It can affect their world views, fill them with hate for others who they perceive as different, like Muggles or Half-Bloods, make them prone to believe stereotypes and feel superior to those they see as fitting into "bad" people categories. It can make them pro-life or pro-choice. It can make them unaccepting of people who are not heterosexual, even themselves. They may be racist or have gender bias.

All these things characters perceive as "truths" can influence their motivation, behaviors and goals. Threshold guardians can use these prejudices to challenge or test the characters. They can be rocked to their core belief systems and discover all they felt to be true was a lie.

They can discover they're a vampire, a shifter, an alien, something they felt didn't exist or something they feel is "bad," as Edward in *Twilight* thought of himself as a monster, a bad guy...*what if I'm not the hero?*

It's very important to know and show your character's belief systems, because it's at the heart of who that character is, who he becomes, and how he gets there.

Naming Your Characters

What would a chapter on YA characters be without a discussion on naming them? It's without question one of the hardest things for many writers to do. In YA fiction, especially, a name can be significant. Names can be relevant to the character's geographic location, time period, ethnicity or socioeconomic circumstances. Your character's name helps define them for the reader and helps the reader identify them. Your character's name is relevant to the story whether you choose a name specifically for its meaning, such as Lang because it means tall, or not.

Geography

You might also have chosen Lang because it's Dutch and the character's parents (don't forget who gives kids their names) or some other relevant character in the backstory came from Holland. If the character lives in Haiti, they probably don't have an Alaskan name. This seems simple, but it's important. Name your characters logically, taking into consideration location. If you deviate from it, be sure you let the reader know why.

If you write science fiction or futuristic fantasy, and the location is another planet or dimension, then you need to come up with otherworldly names like Spock, Chinger or Coreeshi. Try not to choose something so phonetically odd your reader won't know how to pronounce it or will call your character by some silly nickname in their head that will lose the persona you intended for your character. Also try to keep names of characters from a shared universe similar in syllables or sounds so they seem "real" to that fantastical but "real" world you have created.

Time Period

This is basic but important. Use names from the time period in which your story takes place, as well as the location. If you are writing a historical, choose a name from the time period in which your character was born. This gets a little trickier if you are talking far into the future. Then you will have to either make up a futuristic-sounding name like Axton or Azura or use contemporary names if you are writing an apocalyptic novel.

No matter what time period you are writing about, you don't want mundane, boring names, at least not for your protagonist—unless they have a cool nickname that symbolizes the change between who the character was born to and who they became despite that. Stay away from trendy, because in a few years the trendy names will no longer be trendy.

Ethnicity

You can tell a lot about a person by her name, including her ethnicity. There are a lot of Greek girls named Athena, Penelope or Daphne. You wouldn't be surprised to discover a boy named Damarcus was African American or that Maria was Hispanic. These are all names that can help readers identify and keep track of your diverse cast of characters. They might also be perceived as stereotypes, unless that's your intention, if you're not thoughtful about your selections. Just don't get too creative or you will confuse your readers rather than enhancing your character's personality.

Let's face it, Toula was a very cute name for the protagonist in *My Big Fat Greek Wedding*, but Fatoula, the name from which it was derived would be unlikely to make it as a popular name here in the US. That character might have a personal nickname and never want anyone to know their given name. That still doesn't mean you should name them Hitler or Lizzy Borden and make everyone have bad feelings toward them due to the connotation those names bring.

Socioeconomics

Names are artifacts. There has been a lot of research done on both the impact of names on a person's perceived ability and actual success and how culture (Binyamin), religion (John, Mary, Joseph) and education levels (Addicus Rockwell, III) influence name choices made by parents. Your YA characters don't care about any of that, unless it's the cause of a name they hate or feel pride in. But readers from the same background or circumstances as your characters might find your characters' names familiar, if you do your research and give thoughtful consideration to naming your characters.

Nicknames

Now after all that thoughtful consideration and planning, you named your characters and like a lot of kids, they or their friends, or enemies, have replaced that wonderful name with a nickname. It could be related to a sport (Baller), a game (Sniper), or some other hobby or habit, or even their looks (Four-Eyes, Metal Mouth). It could refer to where a homeless kid lives, like "Walmart" in *Voodoo Child*, or what a kid does, like computer guru Web Paige in *The Web Paige Chronicles*. Nicknames can be great fun, and can also be a source of torment, shame and bullying. Choose them wisely.

Diversity

Be sure to keep your characters' names as diverse as the characters themselves. What reader can keep Joey, James, Jimmy and Jeremy straight? How about Brenda, Belinda, Bethany and Beatrice? Vary the syllables too. Names are repeated over and over in stories and you don't want all the names to sound or feel alike.

As you can see, there's a lot of planning and thought that needs to go into naming your characters, especially the protagonists. Use these tips as a guideline but have fun with it. Baby name books and online name generators in any ethnicity you can think of are great ways to get your name ideas flowing. Have fun naming your babies and be glad these kids can't complain about what you named them...unless you want them to.

Chapter Seven

Romance in Young Adult Fiction:
To Kiss or Not to Kiss

The Romantic YA fiction market has declined over the past couple of years as teen readers turn to fiction that's more interesting to them or more dramatic and darker. But a romantic element is almost always something that should be included in your YA book. Kids like to see other kids going through what they go through every day as they fall in and out of love.

The most common question about putting romantic elements in YA fiction is, how far can you go? How far is too far and what about Middle Grade? There are no rules, but you should take into consideration what you know from your experiences, what actual teens say, and what it says in books and articles online.

Middle school kids shouldn't be doing anything beyond a possible chaste kiss in your books. There are exceptions. If you're writing a story about a middle school girl who ends up pregnant, or maybe a clique of wild girls who dress and act inappropriately to attract attention to themselves by acting above their age, you could stress the limits. However, not too many readers of YA fiction are interested in reading about a twelve-year old having sex, and it would be very tasteless to most adults to write it. It might possibly be a topic, or a dark thing that might be happening, but you don't "see" it in the book, possibly, but Middle Grade is and should remain sexless.

YA fiction is almost the same. Teens seventeen and younger just don't need to be having sex in the pages of a young adult novel. Even Bella waited until she was 18, although Edward did tear her baby from her womb with his teeth and then bit her until she died—you had to be there. No, really.

You'll never see teens under 18 having sex in a YA movie unless it's about abuse, drug addiction and prostitution, or some other extraordinary circumstances. In *Save the Last Dance,* there's a girl who is in high school who had a baby, which is fine. It happens. But Julia Stiles's character kisses her boyfriend only once in the entire movie. There's some hugging and dirty dancing, but it's basically a clean movie. Even in *Guardians of the Galaxy*, a movie made from a comic with protagonists over eighteen, the movie is aimed at young adults, so no sex. The *Harry Potter* series, no sex. It just doesn't work. Your characters can fall in love, hold hands and have yearnings, but they shouldn't close the deal. In New Adult, things get steamier, but New Adult features protagonists between 18 and 30 (or so).

Even though YA romances aren't as popular as they used to be, falling in love is one of the most popular topics in YA novels. Falling in love is difficult for teen characters. A teen falls in love and, one minute, the world is rosy, they get dumped in two weeks and everything is dark and dismal. You need to capture those emotions, those ups and downs, the rollercoaster of moods and reactions normal to every parent of a teenager and every teen.

You also want to tell a story with solid pacing and structure. Before you examine the five stages to falling in love and how to craft a teen romance using these stages, here are the 12 stages of intimacy. These are real. This is the progression, the way it almost always goes.

1. Eye to body (check that hot guy out)
2. Eye to Eye (making eye contact, oooh)
3. Voice to voice (Sometimes for a teenage guy or girl just talking to the opposite sex can be difficult, so this is a major step)
4. Hand to hand or hand to arm (Big step that first actual skin contact. This could give a guy or a girl pimples for a week)
5. Arm to shoulder (As in the movies, putting an arm around the girl is huge)
6. Arm to waist (Not much of this goes on with teens)
7. Mouth to mouth (The pinnacle of firsts in almost everyone's life, the first kiss)
8. Hand to head or face
9. Hand to body (Stop here in YA)
10. Mouth to the parts . . .
11. Hand to other parts. . .
12. Actual sex (Just no)

There are stages of falling in love for most teenagers. This can, of course, differ with kids in difficult situations, broken homes, inner city kids, homeless kids, abused kids, and maybe that's what you're writing about, but these are the basic steps.

Stage One: Infatuation

One day everything is normal. Then, in the next moment, your teen characters are thrown off balance by meeting each other. However, don't be fooled. This initial meeting will not be enough to carry your teen love story. In all romance there is one cardinal rule. Conflict. You think of a character, say one who hates lies, and you give that guy a girl who hasn't told the truth in her entire life. There's your conflict. How can these two kids fall in love?

Maybe they are in love, have a relationship and then one moves three-hundred miles away. How do they keep that romance going? A teen romance can't simply be based around two characters who are falling in love. There must be a conflict, whether internal or external, that keeps the two characters apart.

Conflict can occur one of two ways. Your characters may have to battle outside forces who oppose their love, such as in the classic Romeo or Juliet -- or in the novel *Twilight*, in which he is a vampire and she is human. Strangely enough, your two characters may not like each other in the beginning of the book. For example, in the teen novel *Flipped* by Wendelin Van Draanen, Julianna is madly in love with Bryce. Unfortunately, he can't stand her. As the novel progresses, we see Bryce fall in love with Julianna while she decides that she can't stand him. Finally, at the end of the novel, both characters have decided they just might like each other.

Sometimes the two future lovers don't even have a clue they like each other until the end. Like in *The DUFF*. Poor Bianca who has just discovered she's a DUFF asks her friend Wesley to help her. He falls in love with her after they spend time together trying to make Bianca hot, which they eventually do.

When you are creating that first meeting, ask yourself some questions. How do your characters feel the first time they meet? Why are they both in this spot at this moment? What character trait do they each notice about the other? This trait may initially be something physical, but to create a satisfying teen love story, your characters should also notice a personality trait. For example, maybe your teen boy is working with younger children coaching on a ball field. Your teen girl has a younger brother who is playing on the team. She notices how patient the teen boy is with her brother. The girl realizes that she wants to know more about this boy, which will lead them to the second stage.

Stage Two: Flirtation

Your teen characters have met. Now, the flirtation begins. At this point, accidental meetings start to occur. Your teens might "accidentally" run into each other at school, parties, or other social events. As the flirtation progresses, your characters will spend more time in proximity to each other. Perhaps, they might go on a date and the all-important first kiss may happen.

However, before you dive into that juicy first kiss, take a minute to think about first kisses. How many first kisses go as dreamed or expected? How many first kisses are just downright awful? The best "terrible" kiss is in *Jumanji 2: Welcome to the Jungle.* Dr. Smolder Bravestone, who in real life is a nerd, wants to kiss Ruby Roundhouse who is also a nerd in real life. He's always had a crush on her. The kiss goes so horribly wrong, but in the end, Spencer (nerd) tells Martha (girl nerd) that he likes her. Not just in the game, but in real life and they take another whack at that kiss and it works out much better.

As you get ready to write that all-important first kiss scene, consider a few important details. What fears do your characters have about the first kiss? What expectations do your characters have? Are your characters the first to kiss in their social group or the last? Is it a bet or a dare that they will kiss each other? Where are your characters during the moment of the kiss? Is it a planned kiss such as after a date or dance, or is it unexpected in the middle of a rain storm? What happens afterwards? Is it awkward? Is that moment broken by a parent or younger sibling who walks in the room? Carefully considering all of these questions will help you craft a realistic first kiss scene.

Stage Three: Friendship

Your story is moving along, and your teen characters are now progressing in their relationship. At this point, your characters have kissed, perhaps had a couple dates, and are beginning to reveal who they are to each other. Now is the time to include a scene or two in which secrets are revealed. Or, perhaps a long-held judgment is reversed as your characters learn about each other. For example, your female character has always believed gang members are bad kids, but now she's falling in love with a gang member.

At this stage, it's very important to understand your character's motives. One way to understand motive is to know why your characters act and respond the way they do.

Some questions you can ask to explore motive include: What secrets do your characters have? Why do they have these secrets? Who are your character's worst enemies? Why? What single loss has made each of your characters the people they are today? What happened in that loss to change them?

The friendship stage is the heart of your story. This is the stage when your characters are deepening their relationship and preparing for the next stage of commitment. Without a strong friendship, your story will not be believable when the teen characters move into the next level of commitment.

There are a lot of teens who never make it beyond this stage. This is the critical make or break stage, the stage where most couples will eventually dump each other. They discover flaws, or communications break down, someone better appears. There are many things that can come between them and do. Freshman and Sophomore teens in high school will be in many relationships, most short, in a single school year. They're really not ready for commitment, just testing the water.

Stage Four: Commitment

This should only come in older teens, probably seniors or juniors. Younger teens are jousting, taking a run at it, then backing off. Commitment is a huge thing. Sometimes they think they're committed and then, boom, they're not interested in that other person at all and maybe they're gay. Believe it, it's happening more and more.

If at this stage your teen characters are ready to make a commitment to each other, it could mean your characters decide to have sex. Or like in *American Pie*, the guy has decided to have sex. The girl might not be that enthusiastic. Boys are, as always, way more eager to try this out than girls. Like in *Uncle Buck*, the girl might have bought a line of bologna, guy saying he loves her, and then comes to her senses.

Just to make this even more confusing (teens are confused so writing about them can be, too) commitment can also mean your characters decide not to have sex—like Edward and Bella. Whether your characters have sex or not should evolve out of who your characters are, and not as a means of sensationalizing your story. For example, in *Perfect Chemistry* by Simone Elkels, Brittney decides to have sex with Alex because she hopes this will encourage him to leave his gang. There is a motive for Brittney to have sex with Alex and it evolves from the characters and the plot. In *American Pie*, all the kids are seniors, probably 18, so when they all find a partner, even Finch and Jimbo, it's not weird. It's a funny movie and it ends well.

There are other ways teens can make a commitment besides sex. Teen commitment can also mean the characters decide to take a big adventure together. For example, if the story has been about getting ready for a mountain bike riding trip, now the big day has arrived, and the teens are ready to take on that adventure.

At this point in the story, your characters may experience that moment of epiphany, the blinding realization that everything is now different. From this moment forward, everything will be changed. In *Jumanji: Welcome to the Jungle*, when nerd Stanley and nerdess Martha kiss, everything in the story and all the connections between them changes. Even Professor Oberon/Bethany notices the connection. Now they're a team and they can solve the riddles together and get the team out of the game. When they're back in the real world, they've seized this reward. They have a relationship forged on shared experience. How they view the world has changed.

Stage Five: Love

Unlike romances for adults, teen romances do not necessarily have a happily-ever-after (HEA) ending. Some have a happy-for-now (HFN) ending. In fact, most teen romances will *not* have an HEA. Why? The answer to this lies in their age. They're young, they're not ready to stay with one person. Maybe their parents are divorced, and they don't believe in love. Or, when they experienced the epiphany moment or moment of change they are no longer the same people that they were at the beginning of the story, so the two teen lovers are not compatible or even on the same page.

For example, the teens may go to different colleges, move, or sometimes a death may occur such as in Jacqueline Woodson's teen novel, *If You Come Softly.* The important part of the final stage of love is that your teen character has undergone a transformation. Neither character is the same person as at the beginning of the story. Their love for each other has changed them, and the story ends.

If the romance, or love story is just a secondary plot in the main storyline, what happens to them after they connect and have their epiphany might not even be addressed. In *Jumanji 2: Welcome to the Jungle,* you see Stanley back in his nerd body and Martha in hers. They see each other in school and you get the feeling they are together, but you don't really know. Unlike books like *Twilight* where the romance was the most important, central plot in the book, and you know in the end Bella and Edward are together and Jacob is not her choice.

Teen love can be complex. But writing about teen love does not have be an exercise in confusion. If you follow these simple stages of falling in love, you'll be able to capture your characters' emotions while crafting a satisfying story arc.

Teen love comes in different varieties.

Instant Love (a.k.a. love at first sight)

If your YA fiction involves two characters instantly falling for each other the minute they meet... Well, get ready for trouble, because this rarely works out.

The prevalence of 'instalove' in YA fiction is a common complaint from readers and is rarely (if ever) received well. So, if you're planning to include a romantic aspect to your story, you must be sure to develop it thoroughly and convincingly. This comes back to being realistic and authentic in your storytelling. Your characters might feel some sort of strange instantaneous connection. But never present this as immediate love. Kids are smart. They know it's not real and they know it won't work. The lack of reality will turn them off.

Falling in love should be part of your characters' journey and development, not an instant standalone event.

The Love Triangle

Love triangles are the central feature in several YA books. *Twilight* and *The Hunger Games* come to mind, but in the *Harry Potter* series, Rowling wrote one into the friendship of Harry and his two best friends, who eventually got together, while Harry had eyes for someone else. If the natural progression of your story involves some type of love triangle, then you may go for it. But just be aware that this angle has been used over and over again, so unless you can bring something fresh to the trope or it's an essential aspect of your story, it might be a good idea to rethink your romance as cliché and boring.

Mechanics

Chapter Eight

Setting, Timeline, Selecting Your Sub-Genre

Setting and timeline are tied to your sub-genre. If you choose to write urban fantasy, then you may be in a modern city or contemporary setting, but there's some weird stuff going on and that includes magic. There may even be vampires or demons on your horizon, dark gloomy allies, and rain. Whatever sub-genre of young adult fiction you choose to write will help you generate an atmosphere and a setting.

Romance is still a popular YA sub-genre. Even if you choose fantasy or a dystopian world, you're probably going to add a little romance.

The National Library lists these sub-genres for young adult fiction: adventure, chick-lit, contemporary, classicised, diaries, dystopian, family and relationships, fantasy, LGBT, graphic novels, horror, historical, humorous, mystery, poetry, paranormal, romance, science fiction, short stories, and steampunk.

In other words, just about every genre of Adult fiction fits into the YA category. But wait, there's more. One of the number one is the seventh book in a series by Aleron Kong, *The Land Predators,* a Chaos Seed book. This book is listed as epic fantasy, video game fantasy and cyberpunk. So, your first lesson in writing YA is there are no rules for genres. Think outside the box. There are all those genres listed by the National Library and then there's a cyberpunk book on the bestselling YA list, and cyberpunk isn't even a recognized genre. What is cyberpunk? As a writer have you even heard of it?

A google search reveals that *Cyberpunk* is a subgenre of science fiction in a futuristic setting that tends to focus on a "combination of lowlife and high tech," featuring advanced technological and scientific achievements, such as artificial intelligence and cybernetics, juxtaposed with a degree of breakdown or radical change in the social order. Cyberpunk plots often center on conflict among artificial intelligences, hackers, and mega corporations, and tend to be set in a near-future Earth. The settings are usually post-industrial dystopias but tend to feature extraordinary cultural ferment and the use of technology in ways never anticipated by its original inventors ("the street finds its own uses for things"). Much of the genre's atmosphere echoes film noir, and written works in the genre often use techniques from detective fiction. Some cyberpunk novels are *Snow Crash* by Neal Stephenson and *Neuromancer* by William Gibson.

This is the kind of writing that is capturing the imagination of teens. To be a YA writer, you need to understand who is reading it and what they want. Educate yourself.

The *Harry Potter* series is still on bestselling YA lists. Harry never gets old. Another best seller is *The Selection* by Kiera Cass. It's a romance and a takeoff on *Cinderella*. Modern tales, or even dark dystopian fiction using fairytales as the loosely-based plot, are very hot right now. The *Red Queen* is another Cinderella-based book that hit the bestseller list. You must hunt through a quarter of the book to find any resemblance to *Cinderella*, but it's there.

Another recent bestseller is *The Hate U Give* by Angie Thomas. This is a gritty story about an African-American girl who witnesses the fatal shooting of her childhood best friend by the police. When she faces pressure from the community she learns to stand up for herself. There is a movie scheduled. What an amazing selection of books. Look at them and realize, teens want to read everything, the trick is presenting a book that appeals to twenty-first century kids. You have to step up.

So, you know your sub-genre, do your research, make sure the world you create in the setting you choose is realistic and captivating. Your timeline for your book can be now, the future or the past.

Setting

Setting is the stage you create for your characters to play on. It can be as simple as a small town or a high school, or as large as Middle Earth. The important thing is you, as the writer, need to know the details of your setting. You must have a clear view of the setting, a vibrant vision, whether it's real or fictitious. Then, once you know, you need to make that place known to your readers. It's not enough in YA fiction to shrug and say any town USA. The setting must be so vividly created there is nowhere else that story could have happened.

Setting is so important, it can even be a character in your story. Think Hogwarts. To every kid who read the *Harry Potter* series,

Hogwarts was a real place. Hogwarts was so integral to the Harry Potter story, it and its accompanying small town are an attraction, an entire attraction, at Universal Studios Orlando. People pay to go there. Another setting that became so important it was a character is the glade and the maze in *The Maze Runners*. The book couldn't exist without the maze. It was an actual character in the book. That's how important your setting can be so think about it carefully. There are a few points to keep in mind when building your setting and your timeline.

Emotion or Atmosphere

When you want to express an emotion through atmosphere, a general feeling of gloom, despair, happiness, or sadness, think about weather conditions that can create these emotions or surroundings that show a mood. Threatening clouds, rain and night can set the tone for the book as dark and scary. The sun suddenly breaking through these clouds can show a lightening of mood. Flowers and a bright blue sky can convey happiness. Changes in the physical environment can illustrate your characters' mood and set the tone or the atmosphere for your book. It's known as pathetic fallacy. Yes, it's a real thing, using an inanimate object of nature to depict emotion.

In *Red Queen*, it's mud. Everywhere the protagonist, Mare, goes, she's being rained on and slogging through ankle-deep mud. It's depressing. Her life is illustrated as hard and made even more difficult because everywhere she goes, she must wade through mud which is symbolic of how she's struggling with life just as she's struggling with walking around. In the *Harry Potter* series it's often dark, stormy, with lightning and heavy fog whenever there is a dire situation or impending doom.

<u>Physical</u>

This can be divided into natural or man-made environments. Everything your character encounters somehow defines them. Where they live defines them. Is it a farm, a city, a suburb? For teens, often their entire world is school and their room. So, make that room a real place. If a teenager is homeless, living in a shelter or a ghetto apartment, this defines who they are in the world and sets the tone for the story.

In *Save the Last Dance*, Julia Stiles character is a teen who lost her mother and had to move to New York to live with her dad. His apartment is dingy, in a ghetto, and she must sleep on the couch. The tone and atmosphere of struggle and sadness seep from the setting. You understand immediately that she's troubled and her new life isn't what she's used to.

In the opening of *The Hunger Games,* Katniss is hunting in a wilderness forest. This sets the tone of violence. She kills for food. You know she's a hunter, you sense the conflict to come. The first *Star Wars* movie opens with a rebel spaceship being intercepted by the Empire in space. Space is the setting. You know right away, this is big. The scope is huge. Princess Leia is the herald. She leaves her interrupted message in the little robot R2-D2, announcing the adventure is about to begin. It's important to set your book's time and place as soon as possible. If it's as important as the Glade in *The Maze Runner*, or Hogwarts in the *Harry Potter* series, tell your readers about it as soon as possible.

<u>Social Structure and Cultural Aspects of Your Setting</u>

The culture of your characters, even if it's just the mini-culture of a high school, its social structure and details are an important part of your story and your character's makeup. This aspect can have a huge impact on how your character's behavior can drive the story. If your character is ethnic, African American, Hispanic, or Asian, etc., this will impact your story and might even be your story. Each of these ethnic groups have a strong culture and social makeup. If your character is LGBT, the way he or she interacts with the other characters and within the social structure of the world you create will have an impact.

These three important aspects of your setting define your characters and their places in the story. The purpose of setting is to create an environment your reader can clearly see. They need to be able to visualize your characters, see them moving through your setting and understand the action as it happens inside the setting you created.

If you want to write for young adults, you must learn to create a realistic setting using as few lengthy paragraphs as possible. Don't let your love of descriptive prose overtake you. Keep it real but keep it short. Young readers don't have a lot of patience to wade through detailed descriptions. They play high-speed video games and cruise the internet. Too much description can be as bad as too little. Kids will flip over the pages and you'll lose them.

Types of Settings

Setting is the tool a writer uses to bring a story to life in a reader's mind. Every child who reads *Harry Potter and the Sorcerer's Stone* wants to walk the hallowed hallways of Hogwarts and play a game of Quidditch. Rowling created a world so real, so much *better* than the mundane one, kids can imagine themselves inside it, participating in the story.

Certain settings are more attractive to young adults. They seem to gravitate toward fantasy and blended stories than those set in reality. But a well-written book about a subject they're interested in can be in the real world. The important thing in a book based in the real world will be the characters and the believable way they interact in this real world. The readers still have to be able to imagine they're there or might turn a corner and see where there is. The settings will do the heavy lifting to catch a young adult's interest.

Realistic

This is obvious. Your setting is based on the real world. Readers know this world, so you can't fool around with it. Everything should act and react as the reader expects. However, there are many interesting realistic settings. Your book could be under the sea or in the jungle, or on top of a mountain. It doesn't have to be in the suburbs or a city.

Fantasy

This is all on you as a writer. You create your own world, the rules are yours, and the physical characteristics of your imaginary world can be as fantastic as you like. There can be magic, supernatural beings and supernatural landscapes. The laws you create for your fantasy world must stay consistent. The best example is always vampires. If your vampire can't fly on page one, he better not suddenly be able to on page one hundred and one--unless you explain how he has acquired this new skill. Readers are smart and WILL notice.

Blended

The blended world is best illustrated by dystopian fiction. This is where reality took a horrible turn and the lights went out. The real world, like *The Hunger Games*, is still pretty realistic. But Effie's hair and makeup are pure fantasy. The capital of Panem is a blend of reality and fantasy.

Planning a Setting

Most authors set their books in a place they know. Unless you're writing fantasy or a blended story, this is a good thing. You can add details that make the reader comfortable, especially if they've been there. Barry Eisler sets many of his books in the orient. He must have lived for a long time in Japan because his descriptions of Tokyo and the rest of the country are riveting. If you've never been there, by reading Eisler, you will feel like you know the place. Randy Wayne White places all his books in or around Sanibel Island in Florida. If you've been there, his books will seem familiar to you. You will feel comfortable in them.

This doesn't mean can't write convincingly about places you've never seen. You just have to do meticulous research. Read travel journals, look at online vacation photos and photos of local residents of your research location. Read blogs with recipes and other cultural information as well as watch travel information videos about the region.

If you're making up a place that you want to feel exists in the real world, look around you. Know your characters and create what you see and know. Place and setting will shape who your characters are and their behavior. There are a few things to think about before you choose your setting.

Top 10 Things That Will Affect Your Choice of Setting

Locale. This is the place you choose to locate your book. Whether it's in a made-up world of fantasy, or a contemporary city, you place your characters in a location you choose. It's going to affect everything they do and how your reader views your book.

1.	**Time of Year**. The time of year can have deeper meaning than just deciding hey, I'll write this in the summer. Time of year can affect everything from the clothes your characters wear to what holiday is going on. Winter equals Christmas and mukluks. Summer means Fourth of July and bikinis. School is out. In YA, if your teen characters are going to school, your book will have to be placed during the fall, winter or spring. And the school schedule then comes into play. Fall is football, Halloween and Thanksgiving. Spring is baseball and spring break. Winter is basketball, Christmas and New Year's. Most high schools base their schedules around sports and holidays.

2.   **Significant Dates** can also be used, such as the anniversary of a death of a character or real person like in *The Hate U Give,* or the anniversary of a battle, such as the attack on Pearl Harbor. Your character's birthday might be important like in the movie *Sixteen Candles*.

3.   **Time of Day** ~ When you start your book is it morning or night? *Harry Potter and the Sorcerer's Stone* begins in the middle of the night and that's significant. Hagrid and Professor McGonagall in her cat form are watching Harry's uncle's house. *Divergent* begins on a very important morning. The morning Tris is going to choose her faction. This is a time of new beginnings for Tris, so opening the book in the morning is important. Readers associate different things with different times of day, giving the writer an easy way to create a visual orientation in a scene.

4.   **Elapsed Time**. The minutes, hours, days, weeks, and months a story encompasses must be somehow accounted for or the reader will feel confused and the story will suffer from a lack of authenticity. In other words, time has to pass in your world and for your characters. It's important to keep track of it. If you are using a count-down to ramp up your tension, keep track of the days. If a character has ten days to do something or the world ends, don't lose track. Readers are smart. They will notice.

5.   **Mood and Atmosphere**. There are many things that affect the atmosphere of a book and this is one of the most important. If you're writing a horror story, don't place your book beside a babbling brook or a sunny beach filled with laughing children. This seems easy but deciding how to create a certain mood can be hard. It can't rain all the time, but in your book, you can have it rain a lot if that's the mood you want. Dark skies and rain make a gloomy atmosphere. Creepy houses,

bad smells, abandoned buildings, dry deserted landscapes all create a certain atmosphere and mood. *Mad Max: Fury Road* was a great example of unbelievably creepy and horrible. The masks, the music, Imperator Furiosa with her one arm, the wives and the war boys who were obviously sick and needed blood transfusions. The dry landscape and the weird inhabitants added to an overwhelming atmosphere of desperation. So well done.

6.   **Climate**. Climate is linked to the geography and topography of a place, and, as in our real world, can influence events and people. Ocean currents, prevailing winds and air masses, latitude, altitude, mountains, land masses, and large bodies of water all influence climate. It's especially important when you write about a real setting to understand climatic influences. Harsh climates can make for grim lives, while tropical climates can create more carefree lifestyles. If you're creating a fantasy world, you make up the climate to suit the atmosphere you're creating. As in *A Game of Thrones*, in the north, winter is always coming. Never forget climate influences your characters. How they live, what they wear and what they do for a living and for fun is all influenced by the climate. Surfers need sunshine and beaches. Snowboarders need snow and ice. Climate matters.

7.   **Geography**. This refers to specific aspects of water, landforms, ecosystems, and topography in your setting. Geography also includes climate, soil, plants, trees, rocks and minerals, and soils. Geography can even be a character in books where mountain climbing is the subject and the mountain assumes an almost human personality, as though trying to kill the climbers. Or in scuba diving when the ocean becomes dangerous and evil, or surfing when the waves become so large they feel like they're trying to kill the surfer. Geography can pose problems for your characters, as in a Western where your character has to cross the Rockies or push those longhorns across a wide river.

No matter where a story is set, whether it's a small midwestern high school or the beach on spring break, the natural world with all its geographic variations and influences will be part of the story. If you're writing science fiction or fantasy, you can use natural geography, or as in Lord of the Rings, make up your own. The rules of geography and climate will still apply even on an alien planet. The various elements might be different, the minerals in the soil might make the mountains and water a different color. In the Chronicles of Riddick movie, *Pitch Black*, the alien planet is hot and dry with three suns, so it is always light, until an eclipse when the creatures that live underground come out and eat everyone. In science fiction and fantasy you can make up the geography.

8.   **Man-made Geography**. People are everywhere transforming the planet, covering much of it in concrete, building cities and roads. If you're using a real setting in a real place, remember to include the natural and man-made landmarks like dams, bridges, ports, towns and cities, monuments, burial grounds, cemeteries, and famous buildings. If your story is in farm country, make note of grazing land, planted fields, what kinds of crops, barns and house. Barns in some parts of the country, like Pennsylvania, are works of art. If your book takes place in a small town, give it a small-town feel; friendly people, quiet two-lane roads, corner stores and that single stoplight like in *Midnight Texas* by Charlaine Harris.

9.   **Eras of Historical Importance**. If you're writing your YA novel in a historical time period, make sure you know your history and make note of any important events, wars, or historical periods. If you write about 1862, the Civil War will probably be linked to the plot. There's no way anyone in that era doesn't even note that it's happening, or have it impact them and their family in some way. If you pick the middle ages, then the Crusades or the plague might be happening. Usually writers who choose to write in a historical time period are very aware of the events of the time. Just be sure to do your research and

if you're writing YA, understand how children and teenagers lived during those time periods. Kids in the middle 1800s often worked on a farm, rarely got the chance to go to school unless they lived in the city, rarely bathed and went to the bathroom outdoors. City life at that time was dirty, sanitation was underdeveloped, basic infrastructure was primitive. The differences between the wealthy and the poor was magnified.

10.   **Social/Political/Cultural Environment**. Cultural, political, and social influences can range widely and affect characters in many ways. The social era of a story often influences characters' values, social and family roles, and sensibilities. If you want to write dystopian fiction, it's likely some political event, or some massive natural event changed the world we know into an apocalyptic world. You might do like *Divergent* and create an entirely new social system. *The Hunger Games* did this as well. The *Red Queen* series created an entirely new world with new rules and a complex social system.

TV has embraced dystopian fiction. Two shows spring to mind, *Into the Badlands* and *The Walking Dead*. If you need ideas for background and location, watch these two shows. Population is also something to think about. Some places are densely populated, such as Hong Kong, while others are not. Your stories need a specific, yet varied population that accurately reflects the place you're writing about.

For fantasy and science fiction anything goes. Make it crowded like the first *Blade Runner* and *Elysium* or deserted like *Mad Max Beyond Thunderdome* and *The Book of Eli*.

Whatever location, genre or time period you choose to place your YA novel, make sure you think of characters as you create your world. They have to live in that world and function as teenagers. Where you put them is important.

Chapter Nine

Point of View—What Works for You

POV, Point of View, whose eyes are we using?

The first thing you must decide when you sit down to write any work of fiction is your point of view. Who's talking? Whose eyes are you looking through? Point of view, or POV which is the common acronym, is how your story is told, the mode of narration. This is important. It effects the mood, the tone, and the overall immediacy of the story.

In YA fiction, the most commonly used method is first person. If you decide to go with first person POV, you can get into only one character's head, the protagonist. The story will be skewed with only his viewpoint of what happens. It does, however, have the benefit of detailing the feelings and emotions of that one person, making the story feel more immediate, and making it easy to build reader empathy for your main character. But it's also limiting. You can't see your protagonist, watch her, or know her through anyone else's eyes. There are three basic POVs.

1.   **First-person POV uses the pronouns "I" and "we".**

Ex: "I ride my bicycle over the bumpy road, bouncing and hanging onto the handlebars."

2.   **Second-person POV uses the pronouns "you".**

Ex: "You ride your bicycle over the bumpy road, bouncing and hanging onto the handlebars."

3.   **Third-person POV uses the pronouns "he", "she", "it", or "they".**

Ex: "She rides her bicycle over the bumpy road, bouncing and hanging onto the handlebars."

First and third-person POVs are most common, with second-person often reserved for interactive fiction stories such as the "Choose Your Own Adventure" books. One example that breaks the mold, however, is *The Fifth Season* by N.K. Jemisin, in which second-person is used to place distance between the protagonists and their experiences to reflect their state of mind. This is an unusual POV. It's extremely difficult to keep straight, but it's interesting.

Here is a short passage from *The Fifth Season*:

> *The Blackstar is where the leaders of the empire meet to do their leadership things. The amber sphere is where they keep their emperor, carefully preserved and perfect. He wanders its golden halls*
> *in genteel despair, doing what he is told and dreading the day his masters decide that his daughter makes a better ornament.*

This book was well received, made the NY Times Best Seller list and won the Hugo Award for best Science Fiction. Books written in second person are very rare.

First- and third-person POVs each come with two main "sub-modes", so to speak.

1.   **In First-Person Reliable,** the narrator tells the story as they see it from their perspective. This is the more popular first-person sub-mode.

2.   **In First-Person Unreliable,** however, the narrator purposefully deceives readers to serve their own purposes. For an example of unreliable narrators, check out *Gone Girl* by Gillian Flynn. If after reading *Gone Girl* you still don't get what unreliable narrator actually means, don't feel bad. It's confusing on purpose.

An **unreliable narrator** is a character whose telling of the story is not completely accurate or credible due to problems with the character's mental state or maturity. Some literary critics argue that there is no such thing as a reliable first-person narrator since every character is affected by his or her past experiences in the telling of a story, but most first-person narrators attempt to give the most accurate version of the events. An unreliable narrator, however, holds a distorted view of the events, which leads to an inaccurate telling of the story. In other words, the narrator has an inaccurate view of the truth. They think it's the truth, but somewhere in their past, the truth got jumbled and now they believe the jumbled version. Remember Edgar Allan Poe's *The Tell-Tale Heart*? The narrator was completely mad and told the reader that. He murdered an old man and cut him up in a bathtub, then buried him under the floorboards. Yup, certifiable. Genius use of an unreliable narrator.

You see a different version of this in people all the time. You were in the car when they drove into a tree, so you know they were drunk and hit a tree. But somewhere over the years, they decided to believe it was really you driving. And they believe that, and they tell everyone the story based on their skewed view. Unreliable. This can give readers or viewers a chance to offer their own interpretations. In other words, the person telling the story could be lying and giving an inaccurate version. This is kind of like having two kids. One kid knocks over a vase and breaks it. Both kids were in the room. You weren't. So, one kid tells the story and blames his sibling. Is this the accurate version or is his sibling innocent and the kid narrating actually broke the vase?

Third-Person Sub-Modes

1.　　**In Third-Person Limited,** the point-of-view is restricted to one character's thoughts and experiences at a time.

With this sub-mode, which is the more popular of the two, the narrator must be a character in the story. This is the most often used by commercial fiction. It's useful because you can be in different places inside the story, say on the spaceship and on the planet by simply using different characters' eyes to view the different scenes. You have to keep it straight, make definite changes and not drift around into other heads. If you view a scene from more than one perspective at a time, you've moved to omniscient.

2.　　**In Third-Person Omniscient**, an all-knowing narrator relays the stories of one or multiple characters in the same chapter, sometimes in the same scene, and as Larry McMurtry does, sometimes in the same paragraph.

An example would be:

Jean couldn't believe Mary didn't like the hat she'd given her. Why it had cost a fortune, was fashionable, and that particular shade complemented Mary's pink complexion.

Mary ripped the hideous hat off her head. Why did Jean insist on buying her expensive presents, Jean knew she would loathe and then expect her to be grateful and happy?

See? Same scene through two sets of eyes, in two different heads. Omniscient is now considered old fashioned and it is very hard to write it well. They call this head-hopping and it can give readers mental whiplash. Most readers find it annoying. Unless done very well, most editors will make you cut it. It isn't generally received well by editors.

A narrator who shares multiple characters' thoughts and experiences is a true-omniscient, while a narrator whose knowledge is limited to just one character is called limited-omniscient.

Whew! That's a lot to think about, right? If you're feeling a bit overwhelmed, consider how different points-of-view are most often used:

1.   **A first-person POV** is most frequently used in Middle Grade and YA fiction, in literary novels, and in stories in which one primary character takes center stage. *The Hunger Games*, *Divergent* and *Red Queen* are all examples of YA written in first person.

This is used because if you're only in one person's head, you see, feel, hear, only from that one person's POV. It's intimate. Personal. It puts readers directly in the protagonist's shoes, encouraging them to not only see the world through that character's eyes, but to *become* that character for a time. Young adults like this because they feel more connected to the character if they're walking around in their shoes, or head, whichever.

3.   **Third-person POV** is more common in mainstream, commercial, action-filled books. It gives the writer the freedom to be writing two or three-story lines, follow two or three different characters, and see a scene from different viewpoints. For example, if your protagonist gets captured by the bad guy, you can be in the bad guy's head and know why he did it and what he's planning. Then you can change into the protagonist's head and know how he or she feels about being captured, and possibly his or her plans for escaping.

Third-person has more of a visual, film-quality feel. In *Game of Thrones*, the producers of the series like to shift from one character to another, one scene to another in the same episode. They do this every eight to ten minutes. This keeps you watching. Readers and viewers have limited attention spans. They love watching some characters, hate watching others and are interested in maybe two of the four storylines running at the same time in the show. So, they wait for the switch, get comfortable, when it switches again, then they wait for another. The storylines are all connected, and the series beautifully binds them all together with the timeline. Writing is the same. You keep all your characters connected through the timeline, although different characters may be doing different things and in different places.

Choose the mode that feels most natural for you to write and the mode that fits your story best. Simple as that.

Tense

"Tense" refers to verb tense, the tool through which you express action and its relation to time in your writing. There are two types of tense that are most often used in fiction:

1.   **Present tense,** the action takes place in the moment, now.

Ex: I run down the road. I'm tired. My feet hurt. I trip over a log and fall, hitting my head on a rock.

Books: *The Hunger Games, The Handmaid's Tale, Red Queen.*

2.   **Past tense,** the action has already taken place.

Ex: I ran down the road. I was tired. My feet hurt. I tripped over a log and fell, hitting my head on a rock.

Books: *The Maze Runner, Harry Potter* series.

Typically, tense follows a similar pattern to point-of-view. Present tense is more immediate and personal, meaning it pairs well with a first-person point-of-view, while past-tense allows for slightly more distance, making it more flexible. Present tense has an odd feel to it and is not a commonly used tense except in YA fiction where you see more of it. If you read a lot, then open a book written in first person present tense, you might go, holy cow! You might never have seen it before. First person present tense is becoming more and more popular. Although there are signs its use is diminishing in work from established writers, among young writers it is becoming the default choice.

Here are some reasons for using present tense.

1.   **Present tense has more "immediacy" than past tense.** In present tense, the reader is there with the narrator step by step as he changes, so the story's climax can be both more immediate and intense.

2.   **Present tense can contribute to the characterization of a work's protagonist.**   Many of the most successful present-tense novels and stories deal with characters who are intensely in the present. Like Katniss Everdeen, her life is changing right before our eyes. We experience everything she does which gives us, the readers, the same experiences she is having. We know her better because we see her reactions to stimulus, we see how she thinks. As readers, we are Katniss Everdeen.

3.   **Present tense simplifies handling tenses.** Whereas past-tense stories often contain the majority of our language's 12 tenses, most present-tense stories employ only four—the simple present, the present progressive, and a smattering of the simple past and the simple future—and many consist almost entirely of the simple present tense. Using fewer tenses reduces the writer's ability to convey time relationships, but many young readers like this kind of simplicity. For example, when we're writing in present tense, we can simply shift into the simple past when a flashback starts and then return to the present when it's finished.

Disadvantages of using present tense

1.   **Present tense restricts the writer's ability to manipulate time.** Altering chronological order and varying duration both work against the primary purpose of present tense, which is to create the feeling that something's happening *now*. It seems natural to alter the chronology of events in past tense, when the narrator is looking back from an indeterminate present at many past times, but it seems unnatural to do it in present tense, when the narrator is speaking from and about a specific present.

2.   **It is more difficult to create complex characters using present tense.** Although it is certainly possible to create complex characters in present-tense fiction, it's more difficult to do so without natural access to the basic techniques that allow a writer to manipulate order and duration. Without the ability to relate backstory through the past tense, characters can become simple, even generic.

Which verb tense is right for your story? Once again, the best option is always the one that feels most natural for you to write. It is worth noting that past-tense is by far the most conventional choice, however. Because present tense is far less common, it can sometimes feel jarring to readers. This doesn't mean there's anything wrong with writing it, but it's a note every writer should consider when crafting his or her story. There's nothing stopping you from trying a couple to see which one feels best for you, and which one you think best tells the story you're writing. If you hate one, try another. But once you do choose one, be consistent!

Chapter Ten

Language and Sentence Structure for YA and MG Readers

Talking like a teenager isn't as easy as you think. Just saying "like" every other word and using a lot of slang (probably old slang) does not make your writing sound like a teen. How do teens really talk? This is a tough question and maybe not what we need to discuss. A better question may be, what kind of language do teens like to read? Dialogue is an entirely different topic. When writing your narrative, keep in mind this is writing. It's like writing any other kind of fiction, only geared toward a teenager's ear.

Keep your sentence structures relatively simple.

Lengthy sentences with big words won't work. The young reader is more sophisticated than you might think, but beautifully crafted prose is wasted. You're telling a story. Just tell it. And that's how kids think. They're in a hurry and impatient with pretense, so don't give them any.

Give them lots of conversations.

Try to tell a lot of your story with dialogue, but not too much, as discussed earlier. Study good YA novels and get a feel for balance because conversation is a great way to involve the reader in the story. Straight narrative gets old and boring. Large chunks of print, long paragraphs look scary to kids. Give them the white space, the dialogue. Short paragraphs make the action flow faster and much less daunting. The trick is to have a mixture of dialogue and short paragraphs that move the plot and keep the story interesting to teens who know all about communication and its importance in realistic interactions.

Don't dumb your language down or talk down to young adult readers.

The first commandment of YA writing should be: never underestimate your audience. Just because you're writing primarily for teen readers doesn't mean you should change your writing style to 'talk down' to them. In fact, if you do this, they'll notice – and they won't appreciate it. Many YA novels are often a little less 'literary' or poetic, a little more straightforward and plot-driven. Maybe that's why so many people who aren't kids read them.

Don't preach.

Kids read for lots of reasons. Some read because they love the stories, the details, the clarity and personal experiences you get in a book. They want to enjoy it. Text books are for school. Lectures come from their parents. You don't have to be the one to tell them smoking is bad or don't drink and drive. If you want to deliver a message like that use your story. Make your protagonist virulently against smoking because their mother died from lung cancer. Make your protagonist a tea-totaller because his step-father is a mean drunk. Teach with story, not with preachy diatribes.

Don't rely on your own experiences.

If you're an adult author writing for a young adult audience, you need to keep in mind the gap in experience and understanding between you and your readers. And that gap can appear most obviously in dialogue. If you grew up in the 80s or 90s, your experience of being a teenager – and the way you spoke as a teenager – will differ greatly from the experience of teenagers today. And while teens won't be your only readers, they should be the primary audience.

You probably have kids of your own. Look at teenagers. Their lives are completely different in so many ways from the life you lived in high school. Lockers used to be huge. You kept everything in a locker, books, toiletries, snacks. Many of today's students don't even know where their lockers are. They never use them. Everything, and I mean everything, they need for their day is in that backpack they guard with their life. In many classes, they don't even get issued a book. Swallow that one. No books except the ones in the classrooms.

Then there's the cellphone issue. You can almost make a teenager do anything you want by threatening to take it away. This small electronic device is their lifeline, their way to stay connected to the world they view as important, and even as a parent, you're probably not in it. So, take your experiences and sift through them carefully. Most will not fit, so don't even go there.

You might think tripping back through your own young adult years is a great way to get 'in the zone' for writing YA fiction. You're wrong. It isn't. I doubt if you had to skip lunch every day because you were an outsider and terrified of being bullied. I doubt if your best friend was gay. Kids today live in a strange and different world. One where they have drills in case a mass shooter decides to kill all of them.

I bet you had at least one parent at home when you got off the bus. Many kids now have two parents working, so no one is there when they get home, no supervision. You might not have lived in *Happy Days*, but life now for kids is a whole other existence, with a completely different set of experiences. This is especially true when writing your characters' dialogue.

Teenage Dialogue, Trying to Master Kidspeak

Different kids have different speech patterns just like adults. A twelve-year old sixth-grader might have the vocabulary of a college graduate while an inner-city kid might not even speak a language you understand. Then there's accents and slang. Kids have smaller vocabularies, at least some of them do. Middle school kids will have even smaller vocabularies, higher voices. Think of that when you're writing; the high squeaky kid voice. They use a lot of superlatives. They get excited easily, and they can be strangely cold and unmoved at times.

To get an idea of the language and speech patterns of kids, watch a lot of Disney Channel shows. You can probably take fifteen or twenty minutes at a time before your mind shuts down. Unfortunately, what Disney presents is how kids in that age group speak. Disney knows how middle school kids behave and talk. They are also good at high school speak. They nailed Stanley and Bethany in *Jumanji: Welcome to the*

Jungle. When Bethany morphed into the game as Professor Oberon, Jack Black made you believe he was Bethany through speech patterns and actions.

So, go talk to and, more importantly listen to, teenagers. If you don't own one, borrow a neighbor's. Ask if you can listen to your friend's fifteen-year-old while they talk to a friend on the phone. You'll be surprised how little slang and affectations they use in speaking. And don't forget to read books, watch a lot of movies and TV shows that feature modern teenagers.

Overdoing it with Slang

In real life, very few teens speak entirely in LOLs, OMGs and WTFs. Do not overload your dialogue with slang terms you think are cool at the moment. You risk your dialogue coming across as forced and unrealistic. Plus, by the time it's published, that slang will likely already be dated and out of use.

This isn't to say you can't include slang at all. Be careful, it can date your work. In *Jumanji: Welcome to the Jungle,* the team figures out Alex has been in the game 20 years by his use of out-of-date slang. He says, "the bomb" and "get jiggy" and they know. Check out popular YA books like Angie Thomas' *The Hate U Give* for examples of well-written slang in both dialogue and character narration.

When writing fantasy, you might want to make up your own slang. *The Maze Runner* did a great job with that and so did Rowling. Rowling had an entire dictionary of terms only magical people used. The kids attending Hogwarts used many slang terms everyone recognizes. Some of the language in the *Harry Potter* series is merely British words, like *berk* for *jerk* or *crumpet.* Some refer to items in the world of wizardry like *muggles, butter beer,* and the game of *Quidditch.*

The Gladers in *The Maze Runner* had an entire list of slang words. *Greenie* for newbie, *slinthead,* a derogatory term, *klunk* for poop, *grievers* were the monsters in the maze and *shuck* was an expletive.

Making up your own language can add interest. In *Avatar* there were strange words for the natives and the strange creatures. The writers invented an entire language for the natives. If you're writing fantasy or science fiction, this is a great idea. Even if you're writing about a certain group of kids in a school, they can make up their own language.

Some slang words have lived through the tests of time. *Dude* is still used, *bitch*, or even *biatch* is what girls sometimes call their girlfriends. *Freaked out* and *bro* are both good, hot as in hot guy or girl. *Chill out* is still used. *Chillax*, as in *Twilight,* not so much. *Creep, weirdo, freak,* still good. *What's up* is still good. All of this was teen verified. There must be a few more. And these can all change regionally, but these ones are somewhat middle-of-the-road.

Mannerisms

More than language or slang, mannerisms define teens as teens. Girls use more hand gestures when they talk. They laugh more, giggling. Girls are higher energy talkers, hammering words out like a machinegun punctuated with groans and giggles. Guys talk less. Geeks have a language of their own no one's really heard because you have to be in the Geek group to hear it. Girls in the Popular group tend to talk only about themselves. Smart kids use bigger words. Video games do not cater to the dumb crowd but use big words, so gamers might have a larger vocabulary. Girls toss their hair or play with it. Guys might touch their faces more, checking for incoming beards maybe. All groups frequently use different swear words. Don't think they don't. Some teens will make eye contact when they talk to you and some won't depending on their personalities.

Writing for young adults is fun because of the language as well as the topics. If learning how kids speak is a chore to you, don't write it. Teenagers are amazing, versatile creatures. Study them and the strange language they speak before you sit down to write.

Chapter Eleven

Pacing Your Way Through the Sagging Middle

Control is the most important part of pacing in any novel, but particularly in a book for young adults. You can't go spinning off on lengthy trips into poetical prose when you're writing for kids. They'll laugh at you and if it's a book, not their precious kindle or tablet, bam, it hits the wall. To hold the interest of any teen or tween, you need to keep the plot rolling, moving forward. Interesting and exciting new developments must spring from your pages and never stop. Keep those kids reading. Hold the interest of a teenager whose phone just beeped with a new text message. Now if you can do that, you've got some good pacing.

A pacing tool you use from page one is opening lines. When you're trying to pen that next big thing think about how you're going to grab your reader's attention immediately. That's called the hook. The hook is something that captures another's attention, like a great opening line. Here are a few examples of great opening lines.

It is a truth universally acknowledged, that a single man in possession of a good fortune, must be in want of a wife. —Jane Austen, Pride and Prejudice.

It was a bright cold day in April, and the clocks were striking thirteen. —George Orwell, 1984.

Every chapter should have a great opening line, but not every part of a book should be paced the same. As a rule of thumb, adding description and slowing down the pace can create suspense. But as you get to the action, the scenes where the main character's adrenaline and danger level shifts into high, there's less room for description, thought, dialogue, and anything that doesn't contribute to immediate survival. This is where you shorten your sentences, stop using commas and make every word count. Lose the adjectives, forget adverbs exist, and write the action.

Let pacing build and release, build and release. Then ratchet it even higher. Working toward a mini climax at a turning point, and then slowing down again allows the reader to catch her breath. At some point, if you don't release the tension, the reader will grow too weary to care much by the time you reach the climax. There are plenty of books and movies out there that forget the waterhole from *The Writer's Journey* and pretty soon you just can't watch anymore or read.

So, you've passed through the threshold, made it by the threshold guardians and now you're in a more intense stage of the writer's journey, tests, allies and enemies. The second *Jumanji movie* clearly shows this. The team of four in the game make it past the snake in the first big test and find their missing piece which is an ally, a new one, one they need. They make it to the ally's home where we have a classic waterhole scene. One of their new allies, Alex's, strengths is making margaritas. The classic waterhole scene is often a bar. As in *Romancing the Stone*, after Joan and Jack T. Colton escape Zolo, they go dancing and have a drink in a cantina. In *Jurassic Park II* after Alan Grant gets chased by raptors and saved by a kid named Erik, they hide inside a water truck and Erik shares a canned meal with him while they take a breather and talk about plot details you as a viewer need to know. But like the journey says, you can't sit still for too long. The adventure beckons and this is YA, so head 'em up and move 'em out.

In YA fiction, one of the best ways to keep things moving is by throwing everything at your characters. If your team isn't dodging the kitchen sink by now, you haven't succeeded. When the team in *Jumanji: Welcome to the Jungle* leave Alex's house, they have new threshold guardians to fight. These are guarding the only way to Jaguar mountain, helicopters and planes. One of the team members must dive into his skill-set bag and come up with a solution. This is part of the wonder of creating a team in YA. Team members can all have different skills that add to the win. Different personalities add to the excitement. Maybe a romance will bloom between one of the team members. Anything is possible.

If you did your homework and created a complex character with lots of depth, by the middle of the book, your reader will care about the characters, have built an emotional connection to them, which will carry them to the end.

Use conflict to involve the reader in the story. Making a connection with the main character isn't the only way to draw a reader in. Tension can pull the reader into the page, and tension comes from conflict, whether on a large scale or a smaller one, internal or external conflict. The more aspects of conflict you can incorporate (one character against another, a character against himself, etc.) the more you create an involved reading experience. This is where in *Jurassic Park III*, Grant discovers his assistant, Billy, has stolen raptor eggs and the raptors are after them. Grant is mad at Billy (conflict between characters) and they're running from raptors (external conflict.) Or, this is where in the second *Jumanji movie,* the rhinos attack. Or in *The Hunger Games* where the game masters release the wolf dogs with the eyes of the dead tributes. In *The Maze Runner,* this is where Gally loses it and tries to keep the Gladers from finding a way out through the maze even though the grievers are loose. Internal conflict here is with Gally and his friends, external is with the element of the ticking clock; grievers are coming for them.

A ticking clock is another great way to pick up the pacing in any work. If there is a time limit on a task or goal that must be accomplished, the tension is always escalated. The reader can feel the urgency because time is tick, ticking away.

Use the "rule of three" to provide structure. The rule is a tried and true method of introducing an important, probably lifesaving, element into the book so when you need it, it's there and the reader can see it. In *Jurassic Park III,* it's the satellite phone. It's swallowed by the Spinosaurus so when it rings the group is alerted to the animal. You see it in the beginning, then when the Spinosaurus eats one of the members of the team, the one Paul Kirby had given his phone to. The group finds the phone later in a pile of dino poo and uses it in the end to call, on its last tiny bit of battery life, for help.

You've seen that phone three times. You know it will work.

So, your character has made it through the threshold, avoided the guardians, watered at the bar, and now her eyelids are heavy. She's losing steam. You've hit the dreaded sagging middle. How do you fix it? Your story development has failed, you know what the end is, you've conquered the beginning now how do you rev up the middle?

There are several methods. One is to ramp up any internal conflicts, any conflicts between your team members, and/or drop a refrigerator on them and let them dig out. Another is to add a new and exciting character to the mix. Like in *Jumanji: Welcome to the Jungle* with Alex or *The Maze Runner* when Teresa arrives. You can also do it by sticking to the path as defined by *The Writer's Journey*. Your characters should be approaching the Inmost Cave. There will be more threshold guardians, more tests. This is the time to bleed in a little romance and have your team clean their weapons, rearm, check their ammunition for the big ordeal to come.

Ideas for Fixing a Sagging Middle

1.   **Trim Backstory** ~ Many first-time authors include way too much backstory. Some seasoned authors do this too. It's natural; after all the planning that goes into the story-crafting process, authors want to tell readers as much as they can. Also, especially in the beginning, they are "getting into" the stories and getting acquainted with the characters. Unfortunately, it can interfere with the novel's present events, or stall the pacing. If past events hog the focus of too many passages, readers can lose sight of the actual story.

2.   **Scrap Dialog** ~ Dialog is essential to a novel. However, first-time authors tend to rely on it too much, almost as if they were writing a play and not a narrative. YA novels tend to contain a lot of it, as a pacing device. A common mistake is writing long, multi-page swaths of endless conversations. These cumbersome, attention-sapping passages can weigh down your plot. Make sure what is said is concise and moves the plot forward.

3.   **Keep Adding New Obstacles, New Challenges** ~ Don't let the pacing lag. This is simple. Add a character, a new danger, a dramatic cliffhanger, or a lightbulb moment that triggers a new opportunity. If you already have these elements in your draft, have them fall on chapter endings to keep readers moving to the next chapter.

4.   **Get Secretive** ~ Give your main character a secret. It doesn't necessarily have to be a shameful, dark, or dirty secret, but something that causes tension. It could be as small as a piece of information the character has to keep close to her chest—letting it get out would be a

disaster. This is also a good way to reorient the *plot* to your *story*. Thomas had dreams in *The Maze Runner*. He knew things about WICKED he kept secret. Thomas's secret came out in the end to help the Gladers escape the maze.

5.　　　**Raise the stakes** ~ You need to make the stakes of your characters' challenges high enough to keep the action moving. Don't let them off easy. Don't be afraid to hurt them, push them, make them work for their reward. Always make life more difficult for your main character. Take a look at your protagonist's key moments throughout your novel. Like inside the game in *The Hunger Games*, the game managers kept throwing new challenges at the tributes. If there wasn't enough killing to satisfy them, they added external trials, like fire and giant dogs with creepy eyes.

In a way, the people who understand The Hero's Journey the best are the makers of video games. Each level has a guardian to get through to get to the next level. The degree of difficulty ramps up as the gamer gets through each level until the gamer hits the top level and the worst, meanest, nastiest enemies and challenges will try to keep the gamer from claiming his reward.

Chapter Twelve

Endings

So, you got off to a great start in your YA novel, hooked your reader with that high concept, propped your sagging middle, followed The Hero's Journey through the black moment and are staring at the endzone but have no idea how to end your book.

Endings are crucial. Try to know how your book will end when you start. The reason there is a sagging middle is most writers know how they want to start and know how they want their book to end, but it's the getting to that end point they struggle with. But sometimes the characters made you change the storyline, or add some important element, and now the ending, even if you knew what it was going to be, has changed.

Writing a satisfying ending is one of the most important aspects of YA fiction. Adults read it because they crave a story with a happy ending, or maybe not happy, but satisfying. Think of all the *Harry Potter* books. Harry always wins over Voldemort. You can TRUST Rowling to save him in the end. That kind of trust makes the read enjoyable. There are ups and downs, but you know in your heart Harry will prevail in the end. In a way, it's why so many people watch television thrillers like *Seals* or *Criminal Minds*. They know the bad guy is going to get it in the end. They know their favorite character isn't going to die.

Young adults reading about people they've grown to love over the course of the book don't want to see them die. If, in your black moment you want to murder someone, pick an important character, but not a character the reader is attached to. And make that character's death mean something. Make their sacrifice worth the reward it brings.

Looking at the first book in *The Hunger Games* series, Rue dies, but her death is what starts the revolution and creates the Mockingjay hero, so her death was a sacrifice that had meaning. Then there's the black moment when Peeta and Katniss are both holding the berries and are prepared to die together. The reader is sure it's all over, but they are saved. The reader sighs with relief and melts into a puddle of ecstasy as the hero and heroine return to the real world with the elixir.

The elixir in *The Hunger Games* is the joy of their victory, but it is also a victory for Panem. As the Mockingjay is born, President Snow kills Seneca Crane by locking him in a room with a bowl full of poison berries. The reader knows Snow killed him because Seneca created the Mockingjay by saving Peeta and Katniss. Now that's a satisfying ending.

In *Matilda,* Matilda's parents give her to Miss Honey and move away to avoid prison, and Miss Trunchbold gets hers. Another satisfying ending. The final book of *The Lord of the Rings,* it's when

Samwise helps Frodo return the ring to the fires of Mordor and the two hobbits get to go back to their homes.

If you're looking for a satisfying way to end your story, take the bad guy out in a spectacular way. Everyone loves to see the bad guy suffer. The theater erupted in cheers when in *Avatar*, Neytiri kills Colonel Quaritch and saves Jake and the entire planet of Pandora. It's epic. There's nothing like a good ending, seeing the bad guy punished for being evil. It's the classic ending for comic books and movies based on them. It's why people read.

Revenge novels are eternally popular. Look at the *Punisher, The Equalizer,* or fairytales like *Cinderella* where the evil stepsisters have to watch *Cinderella* marry the prince. This is one of the reasons books, like *Red Queen* by Victoria Aveyard and *The Selection* by Kiera Cass, loosely based on fairytales are so popular.

Here are some basics everyone should know about endings.

1.   Effective endings show (or suggest) the result of the story's conflict.

The conflict of a story is a problem that the main character must solve.

Examples of story conflicts:

- Prim is picked in the Reaping so Katniss has to volunteer to take her place in *The Hunger Games.*
- Thomas is thrust into the Glade with a maze to figure out in *The Maze Runner.*
- Frodo is given the ring and told to get it out of the Shire.
- Mikey and Brand's parents are losing their home in the *Goonies,* so Mikey has to find One-Eyed Willy's treasure.

Readers keep reading to find out if the character will succeed in solving this problem. Is Katniss going to survive the games? The story conflict gives readers a reason to turn pages. At the end of the story, readers expect a payoff. Your story has raised a question, and readers want to know the answer. Some story endings supply this answer in a tidy package. Cinderella marries the Prince, and they live happily ever after.

Many other successful endings only hint at the result of the conflict and trust readers to fill in the blanks. YA readers want the complete ending. They want all the blanks filled in. Don't leave them hanging and don't kill off a protagonist the reader has just suffered with through three hundred pages on the last page. Just don't. When you're writing a series, you can leave questions unanswered in the first or second books but give your reader some reward for reading. Getting young adults to read is hard. If you torture them with a dramatic death of a loved character at the end of your book, they might never pick up a book again and probably won't read any more of yours. Trust has been broken and with young readers trust is everything.

If you don't know what the main conflict in your book is, work on that before you worry about an ending. Often when writers don't know how to end their stories, the real problem is they haven't developed a clear story conflict. They need to go back and work on the beginning and middle of their story. The right ending depends on what comes before it.

2.   Effective story endings come from the main character's actions.

For example, when Peeta and Katniss decide to die together to end the games, that decision and their following actions, create a satisfying ending. When Harry Potter goes through the trapdoor to find the Philosophers Stone, his decision and his actions along with his friends, Ron and Hermione, create a satisfying ending. Sam's decision to accompany Frodo into the world of adventure in the beginning of The Lord of the Rings story is what, in the end, leads to a satisfying conclusion.

Story endings are more satisfying when the main character makes them happen. The character confronts a conflict with his/her strengths and weaknesses. Maybe he or she will win the battle. Or maybe too many odds are stacked against success and everything will end in failure. Either way, the reader is there to watch the confrontation and will be disappointed if it feels like you've fixed the fight.

3.   Satisfying story endings use elements from the story's beginning and middle.

Imagine a novel where your characters are running from the bad guys through space. The black moment arrives, and the hero is killed, but at the last minute, a character is invented by the writer who gives his magic life force to save the hero. Hurray, right? No, not hurray. This manufactured ending is just that: manufactured not created through careful plotting. All you had to do to fix this and make it rewarding was to introduce this character somewhere in the middle, let the reader know about their magic power with events that show it. This is usually done using the Rule of Three. If a reader sees this character do three magic acts, when you save the hero at the end by using his skill, the reader will believe, satisfaction is attained. Three is the magic number.

Even a twist ending, designed to surprise the reader, should not come out of the blue. A great twist ending makes readers see the story beginning and middle in a different light. They remember seeing those magic acts three times and their disbelief is suspended.

This *aha* moment comes when the reader realizes afterward that the seeds of the surprising ending were in the beginning and middle, even though he or she didn't recognize them at the time.

Think of the famous twist at the end of the movie, *The Sixth Sense*. The boy sees dead people, right? The viewer knows this so at the end, when the audience understands Bruce Willis is dead, they are surprised but not shocked because throughout the movie, the writers carefully inserted clues to show he was dead. Best twist story ever.

Remember that, as an author, you can "cheat" to set up your story ending. Once you know how you want the story to end, you can go back and plant hints here and there for the reader, so that when they reach your ending it will feel logical and inevitable.

4. Don't Forget Your Hero.

This may seem obvious, but writers have violated this. Your lead character should be center stage at the end. Everything he learned throughout all the complications that arose from his trying to fix the terrible conflict should by now have made him that guy: the person who rises to the occasion.

Maybe to this point he has been flawed, weak, defeated. But his character arc is about to resolve and become complete. This is what makes a reader respond emotionally, and if it moves you when you write it, it will move your readers.

5. Great story endings make the reader feel something.

If you bring your characters and conflict to life, readers will care how everything works out and will feel something when your character succeeds or fails.

Experiment to get the most emotional impact out of your ending. Try ending your story a little sooner; try ending it later. Try phrasing it differently. Push the words around until you get the spark that makes the magic happen.

Keep the End in Sight the Whole Way

Don't play the wishing game, hoping it will simply work itself out when the time comes.

Whether you're a meticulous plotter or write by the seat of your pants, have an idea where your story is going and think about your ending every day. How you expect the story to end should inform every scene, every chapter. It may change, evolve, grow as you and your characters grow, but never leave it to chance.

Remember, Nothing Can Follow the End

Too many beginners think it appears sophisticated to leave things nebulous, or they want to save something crucial for the Epilogue. Avoid that mistake.

Young readers raised on television and movies like chronology—beginnings, middles, ends. They expect the end to do its job.

Chapter Thirteen

How to Craft a Young Adult Series

The series has become the stellar work in young adult fiction, the star every author reaches for. Who hasn't read a book, loved the characters, and died inside when it was over, only to spring into life when you discover the author is writing a series and a new book is coming out? Oh, the joy, when you realize you get to spend more time with the characters you love (or hate) in the created world in which they live.

There are many wildly successful YA series. The whole series thing seems like it began with *Nancy Drew* mysteries by Carolyn Keene. That series continued until 2003. Talk about long-running young adult books. *The Hardy Boys* books came out even earlier in 1927, were revised in 1959, and in 2005 became another series, *The Undercover Brothers*, which ran until 2012. That series was written by a host of ghostwriters. *The Black Stallion* series by Walter Farley came out in 1949 and became a twenty-book series. Then there was the *Harry Potter* series. Kids lined up on the streets waiting for the next book to come out. How many adults ever thought kids would want to read a book? J.K. Rowling became an overnight success.

There are too many series books to list all of them. You know the ones that made it into the movies: *Harry Potter, The Hunger Games, Divergent, The Maze Runner, The Chronicles of Narnia, The Black Stallion,* and even *Little House on the Prairie*. We've all read these series books and loved them, but how do you write one?

First, writing a series of books that capture the imagination of young adults is difficult and daunting. There are two kinds of series books. One has a story arc that's too big for one book and is fleshed out over multiple books. The second kind is the self-contained, episodic series of stories that resolve by the end of the book and follow the same cast of characters usually with one central protagonist. There are of course variations of both.

The first variety, the story that got so big it could only be told in a series, is easily recognized in *The Hunger Games*, a well-planned series based on a huge story. *The Lord of the Rings* was an enormous story with a huge scope. Middle Earth was a carefully crafted world with enough room for even more than Tolkien's one story. Writers have created very successful fan fiction based in Middle Earth. *The Grey Bastards* by Jonathan French is just one.

Some of the books written as a series give you the feeling the story might not have been planned to be that huge. Perhaps the success of the original book prompted the writer to extend the story into a series, or maybe they were pushed by the publisher. The end result is a series that doesn't capture your imagination, might feel forced, or is based on such a small concept, you lose it in the jumbled writing. If you want to write a series, plan it that way. Create a story big enough to fill three books. If you write one good book and then try to wing number two, readers will know.

The second variety of series books is a book that can stand-alone, usually with one central character in each one. The first series written this way that comes to mind is the *Jack Reacher* series by Lee Child. Child has written twenty-nine Reacher books, all best sellers, two translated into movies. For young adults, the *Throne of Glass* is so far, a seven-book series, featuring a female protagonist Celaena Sardothien in what the author, Sarah Maas, describes as a Cinderella-type story. Each book is centered around the one protagonist. The *Harry Potter* books are all stand-alone novels featuring the central character, Harry Potter.

This second kind of book series doesn't have to be read in order. You can grab one at a time and it will satisfy as a complete novel. If you're writing this kind of novel, especially with one character as the center, this character better grow, develop and change. The first *Harry Potter* book could have fallen into the Middle Grade category, but by the last one, Harry had grown into a young man, changed, learned skills, fallen in love and so had his friends who all proceeded along the journey with him, and the books were solidly young adult.

So how do you write one of these fantastic series?

1. **Make sure you have enough story.** As mentioned before, there are very successful series out there that feel like they were forced. You don't want your reader to toss book number three against

the wall two chapters into it, because they've had enough, their attention wasn't captured, their disbelief wasn't suspended. You need to begin with enough content to justify more than one book. You have to have a complex world with a huge story. And remember, just because you have a lot of room to write, don't bore your reader with unnecessary scenes and passages just because you have plenty of room, and don't freak out if you think you don't have enough content and start padding your book with extra scenes or material that don't progress the story.

When you plan each book, you must think about how you're going to end it before you get there. You could, like Tolkien's *The Two Towers,* just drop your reader with an unresolved situation, leaving them running like gazelles for the bookstore, or heading for Amazon® to download that next book. It's perfectly okay to have the greater plot unresolved. You know it can't be resolved until the end of the series, so figure out a way to end each of your series books with some small success, some forward progress, so the reader has a satisfying experience, and moves to the next book excited to follow the characters and discover the plot resolution, but not panicking as they worry about their favorite character abandoned on a hill being overrun by orcs. If you drop your reader like this, they won't trust you.

Some readers fall so far in love with the characters in your book they want to follow them on Facebook. They want to know what happens next, now that you've given them a new life. Maybe they're not sure the characters will really live happily ever after or they see possible problems cropping up and want to know how their favorite protagonist is going to handle them.

It's the author's job to plant these questions. You can do this through amazing characterization. Or you can do this by creating a plot that's big enough to take multiple books to resolve.

George R.R. Martin, author of *The Game of Thrones*, not a YA series but one that everyone knows something about, had his own formula for keeping the reader interested. He killed off the characters you loved, admittedly a unique idea, and kept the ones you hated alive and thriving. He did this hoping and assuming you'd keep reading just to see the bad guys get theirs in the end. And it worked. The series and TV show have millions of followers. Everyone is waiting for that last episode on HBO®, so his formula worked. He thought outside of the box and achieved great success. You can, too.

2.   **Planning is Everything.** If you're writing the one gigantic story in the three-or-more-books kind of series, you need to lay out a complex plot outline, know where each book is going to end, who your characters are, and your created world. If you don't have your plot carefully planned using the Writer's Journey story arc to cover the entire series, it won't work, and you'll create holes. Readers will know you left something out, skipped an important subplot or forgot it altogether. Readers are smart and the ones who are following your storyline and your characters will know them as well as you do. They are:

- Ordinary World to begin the series
- The Call to Adventure that is the inciting incident and gets your series rolling.
- Refusing the Call has to be in there to tell the reader it's dangerous, different and exciting.
- Enter the mentors, the team members (e.g., Ron Weasley and Hermione, Samwise, Pippin and Merry, Gandalf.) This is where you introduce the characters who will carry this series to the end.
- Crossing the First Threshold must exist in the first book of even a large series. Harry had to go through platform nine and three-quarters and board the train. Frodo had to set out on his journey,

Katniss and Peeta had to climb on the train to the capital. Every hero and his/her mentor must set out on the journey.

• The remaining books will be filled with the testing, enemies, making friends, fighting battles with small victories and successes to take the reader to the next book in the series. Katniss and Peeta survive the 74th Hunger Games, only to be plunged into the games again in book two.

• The last book will begin the wrap up. Each book may have a small black moment, as in when Katniss and Peeta are poised to swallow the poisoned berries, but the true Black Moment, the biggest one, will come in the last book.

• The Reward for Katniss and Peeta is peace and a world without President Snow or President Coin.

3. **Check and Recheck, Study Your First and Second Books.** This is critical. You must know everything about your characters. Fill out a character detail sheet for every character that continues through the series. Know their language, their motivations, their weird quirks and habits, their personalities. Keep them the same. These characters can grow and mature. They can achieve their personal goals as they work to achieve the main goal of the series, but their basic looks and personalities should remain consistent. As you write, you need to check and recheck this to make sure you have no inconsistencies. Katniss can't suddenly become a wimpy crybaby. No one would buy it and it would ruin the story.

4. **Series Timeline.** Believe it or not, this can be the most complicated part of writing a series. You have to keep the seasons, the passing of time, the legs of the journey, the years consecutive, in order.

When you start writing book two, you need to think about when it begins as well as where it begins. Maybe the timeline has advanced ten years. Your characters are older, more mature. Or maybe you drop them in a month after the last book ended. Get your readers up to speed with an appropriate lead-in. Don't bore the reader with rehashing too much of the previous story, but through careful use of characters and dialogue, you can gently get the reader back into the story while you make them aware of where the story is going in this book.

If you are a new writer, it's important to get book two out as soon as possible so the readers don't forget you or your book. Time is passing. New books are grabbing their interest. Get your book done and get it to your readers.

5. **Don't Just Tell the Same Story Over and Over.** This is self-explanatory. Girl gets in trouble, girl gets out of trouble by being a superhero, with her charm and wit and, of course, sarcasm. I'm already asleep. Lee Child does have a formula for most of his *Jack Reacher* books that could fall into the same thing happening over and over category. Someone is mean to Jack or does him wrong, he gets into a fight, gets mad, gets even, solves someone else's problems on the way. But because you love Reacher, you keep reading. In a way, the *Harry Potter* series skirts this formula. Harry gets in trouble, uses his magical power and the help of his buds to save the day and Hogwarts and all the witches out there. Most of us love Harry and his friends so much, we don't care. And Rowling put so many new and interesting problems in his way, it stays fresh. That is the power of characterization. Create a wonderful protagonist, a unique and loveable character, and your readers will want to read every book written about that character. *Nancy Drew* and *The Hardy Boys* series were all exactly the same, but you loved the characters and didn't care.

6. **The Middle Books Will Be the Hardest.** If you're writing a three-to-five-book series, like *The Hunger Games, Divergent, Percy Jackson and the Olympians* books, *or The Maze Runner* series, you can run into middle-book syndrome which is reminiscent of the sagging

middle, something that happens to stand-alone books. You're not in the last book where everything gets wrapped up, you have the big dark moment and tons of action. You're stuck in the middle and have to figure out a way to keep the story moving and hold your reader's interest. The middle books can get muddled, be slower-paced and full of filler.

If you remember each book must contain its own story arc, use the second book to develop your characters, shed some light on their motivations and bleed in more backstory. You can make the second book as great as the first by adding new characters or even a new protagonist as long as the storyline is the same. Remember pacing. Keep it as action-packed as you did the first and create an ending that both satisfies the reader and foreshadows what's to come in book three.

7.   **Create an Antagonist You Can Keep Forever.** Think of Darth Vader and the Empire, Voldemort, President Snow, The Machines in *Terminator* movies or the aliens in *The 5th Wave*. If you create an antagonist so mean, so hateful and frightening, it will last the series. Just don't kill the antagonist off in book one. Make him or her really hard to get rid of. A truly terrible bad guy can carry a story almost as well as a really wonderful protagonist. As Martin knew when he created the *A Song of Ice and Fire* series (*Game of Thrones*), hating the bad guys can keep the series rolling just as well as loving the good guys.

8.   **Keeping Track of the Details.** When you're writing a book series, you need to have a clear understanding of the world you created for your characters. This could be like *The Hunger Games*, which has an entire government, districts, different kinds of people living in different parts of this world. It could be as complex as Middle Earth or as small as the complicated world of North Shore High School in *Mean Girls*. When you're writing a series, each of your novels will

probably exist in the same world. So, create a file that tracks the following:

- What's the physical description of the world?
- What types of people live there (how do they look, how do they dress, what are their beliefs)?
- What type of language is spoken there?
- What's considered normal?
- What are social classes and how do they engage with each other?
- What do they believe about wealth, poverty?
- What type of government do they have?

As said previously: details, details, details. Make sure you keep them straight.

9.   **Know When to Call it Quits.** Not every story needs a sequel, prequel, different angle, spin-off, or to be made into an entire series. Some of the greatest stories stand alone. By forcing a sequel (especially if that sequel wanders around lost and has no clear objective) you can sour the readers and dissuade them from ever buying another book that you write. That's not what you want, so be sure that you have a compelling reason to go with a book series.

If you choose to write that series, know when to end it. Have your plot worked out so there is a way to end the story satisfactorily. You'll want to wrap up all your storylines, all your character arcs in one nice package, tie it with a bow, and say "Done!" And just from us to you, please don't kill off the main protagonist in the last book. Just don't.

The Business

Chapter Fourteen

Concept; Go High

You're probably thinking that high concept in writing YA should mean a book with a theme about something meaningful that will make teenagers better people and give them an important message they can use in their daily lives. It can be a book like that, but what high concept really means is something commercially viable--a book that will translate into a blockbuster movie and make zillions of dollars, another *Harry Potter* book, please, or *The Hunger Games.*

That's what agents want to see. They want your high-concept pitch. And by the way, there's no such thing as low concept. There are a lot of "B" movies most of us would call low concept. *Shoot 'em Up*, a surprisingly entertaining movie, was nothing but gratuitous violence involving, of all things, a baby and carrots. It was probably not pitched as a high-concept thriller. It did turn out to fit the bill in both aspects. It made money and there was a theme with a message. Go figure.

Larry Brooks of Storyfix.com defines high concept as a story that stands out "among a pile of manuscripts that...are well written and well populated with compelling characters," by "glowing in the dark." High concept is all about making your story so good it literally glows and every agent and editor will want to sign it. It's a story that involves something everyone can identify with and has a built-in audience but turns that something on its head or gives it a creative twist while also providing a sense of complexity and richness that can continue past one book.

Easy, right? Ugh, no way.

Jay Schaefer, the editor who produced *Under the Tuscan Sun*, says, "Everybody's looking for the next big thing -- a work of great . . . fiction from an unknown writer."

Try to include as many teen archetypes and characters as fits the narrative. The readers will surely find one who reminds them of someone, or one that they wish was their best friend.

1.   **Recognizable ~** Build a world most teens will find familiar; like high school or the horror of breaking out in zits on prom night. Maybe give your teen parents from hell. All kids can relate to that. The *Harry Potter* series had the Dursleys. Matilda's parents were awful. In *Despicable Me*, the three girls lived in an orphanage run by Miss Madison Hattie (mad hatter) who put them in the box of shame. Even Gru was better than Miss Hattie. Maybe a teacher is the recognizable authority figure they'll love to hate, like good old Miss Trunchbold from *Matilda* or Principle Rooney from *Ferris Bueller's Day Off*. Most teens participate in some kind of extracurricular activity or sport. That could be the recognizable part of their world. In *Coneheads*, Connie

Conehead is a cheerleader. There she is, weird and pointy-headed, but normal at the same time because you recognize where she fits in. What you're striving for is a built-in audience. A story so recognizable, everyone understands it.

2.   **Twistable** ~ This is harder to explain. You take two threads, maybe two protagonists, or even three, and twist them together to make one story. Think of the *way Game of Thrones* takes all those characters, gives you a ten-minute scene with one, then switches to another. It's all those separate stories, twisted together so it makes one.

Attention spans are the shortest ever in history because of electronics, TV, computers, and iPhones. Teens are used to instant gratification and layers of the storyline using the different characters keep your interest. Some characters may be important for the storyline, but you're not that invested in them, so you get some popcorn or follow while texting your friend, then when your favorite character comes on, snap back to attention. HBO is a master at this technique. Other series shows, like *Ray Donovan,* also use this technique. Showtime® also uses this on its blockbuster hit, *Outlander.* Movies are big about this, *Jumanji: Welcome to the Jungle* switched back and forth between characters, twisting their threads into one plot. *The Lord of the Rings* movies also used the technique to great effect. J.K. Rowling did this in later *Harry Potter* books. The earlier novels were all about Harry, but Rowling ran with the storylines of other characters later in the series.

3.   **Relatable** ~ Make your YA story relatable to as many teens as possible. Not all kids will find themselves in the characters of your story, but they should recognize them as people they know or would like to know.

Another way to twist the story is to get your readers headed in one direction and then do an about face and go back or in a completely new track. Rowling used this technique in later stories as well, and she introduced time travel in *The Prisoner of Azkaban* by using time-turners. This kind of flashing back in time was a serious twisting of the plot. It enabled Harry, Ron and Hermione to rescue Hagrid's hippogriff. Another huge plot twist in a book is in the second book in *The Hunger Game* series, *The Hunger Games: Catching Fire*, when at the end Katniss is whisked out of the games by District 13, a supposedly poisoned and abandoned district, and Peeta is captured by President Snow's men. Another huge twist in *The Maze Runner* is when Thomas and the Gladers finally escape the glade to discover they are being manipulated by WICKED. It's these surprising plot twists that make a book, a show or a series high concept.

4.   **Layerable** ~ To make your book high concept, you have to add layers. *Star Wars* is a great example. The characters carry the main job of layering. The movie follows Luke, Obi-Wan Kenobi, Princess Leia, Darth Vader and Han Solo all at once by using the technique of layering. They smoothly move from scenes covering on character to another.

This layering is what gets twisted into one strand of story. You have more than one plot, each connected to the goals and motivations of each character. You have Luke discovering slowly, by inches, who his father is. You have the budding romance of Luke and Leia, and Luke's growing knowledge of the Force. The goals and motivations of Darth Vader and the Empire colliding with the goals and motivations of the Rebel Alliance. All with Obi-Wan circling and spiraling through each scene, first as a living Jedi and the later as a ghostly mentor. Then more layers are added in subsequent movies by adding more characters. This story is made high concept by all of these different layers.

Sometimes this idea of layers can be an overlaying plot running through the story, which is not seen but understood. For example, through all the *Harry Potter* books, Voldemort is there, a shadow hanging over everything, an unresolved problem, a dark presence. *Star Wars* is the same. No matter who's in the spotlight, the overwhelming presence of the Empire hovers above everything. *Outlander* is another example. No matter how happy Claire and Jamie are now, you know eventually they will be torn apart. Claire will return to her own time and Jamie will remain in his. All the storylines beneath that twist and turn making *Outlander* high concept.

5.   **Expandable** ~ This point is self-explanatory. Expandable means it can be made bigger whether through more books or by making the story bigger. Agents and editors are looking for that blockbuster book they can make into a series because the more books, the more profit. The publishing industry is a business, and they're always hunting for the next big thing they can make even bigger.

Comic book series have changed the movie industry. *Spiderman, Superman, The Avengers, Iron Man, Batman, X-Men, Guardians of the Galaxy*, all of these hit movies were comic books. Huge ideas and high concept often come from comics. Many people acknowledge that Neil Gaiman's *Sandman* Series, nearly all his stories, use a Hero's Journey concept. He's well known as a master of *The Hero's Journey* by Joseph Campbell.

Comic book authors create amazing superhero characters who could last through many different movies. It all goes back to great characters on a hero's journey. Creating a wimpy kid and his diaries, creating two star-crossed lovers being zapped through time, mutants saving the world, all character-driven stories: all, in their way, are high concept.

High concept translates to commercial. A commercial book is one with blockbuster potential. This potential could come from a trendy genre or topic, an engaging world that captures the interests of a young generation like *The Hunger Games* or *Red Queen*, or a spectacular character like Katniss Everdeen or even a "meets" book. A commercial premise like *Matilda* meets *Harry Potter*, or *Vampire Academy* meets *Buffy the Vampire Slayer.* These ideas get a lot of editor attention, which makes them high concept.

Chapter Fifteen

What Editors and Agents are Looking for in YA

Editors and agents want whatever publishers want. Their recommendations and thus their reputations depend upon being able to detect outstanding manuscripts with an edge that will set them apart and still cater to a lucrative portion of the marketplace. That's what publishers want.

Most effective agents want whatever editors currently want, because editors will be pitching stories to publishers. Agents make sure to stay on top of the market and talk to editors, so they know what those stories will be.

Did you read the last chapter? Good, then you have a fairly good idea of what editors and thus agents are looking for. If you are reading this book, you probably want to write YA fiction, and that's good too because it's selling, and its fan base is growing. As discussed earlier, it's also fun to write. It's holding the lion's share of the current book market and shows no signs of slowing, even in the face of dismal sales in adult fiction. YA books being published have increased 120% in the past decade.

YA fiction is hot now because the largest group of readers likes to read it. They read more books than any other age group, so they buy the most books and thus generate the most money for publishers and the book industry. That group is the Millennials. Add the obvious group of YA readers, teens, and you begin to get a picture of why YA is flying off bookshelves--entire bookshelves. These buyers like the paperback editions. And all independent bookstores say thank you as they stock as many YA books as possible. This is also why the Big 5 are still offering sizeable advances for this genre, and why as discussed previously even the biggest bestseller authors are being urged by their editors and fat advances to participate in this market.

You must be aware, however, that because this is such a popular market the competition is fierce. If you utilize the information and ideas in this book, it should help level the playing field, but to get a manuscript that glows, illuminated above the ever-rising stack of author hopefuls, you need to have an edge. That immediately disallows the done-to-death, we-are-so-sick-of-this tropes, like the *ménage a trois*.

Acquisition editors are looking for stories with characters that suck them in from the first line and take them on a roller-coaster ride that will leave them breathless and deeply moved--and it's not easy to move an editor. A fun pastime for good writers at a book fair or conference is to go around opening books and reading the first sentence. Then they discuss what it might be about, what it makes them wonder, and if it intrigues them. Only then do they read the back-cover blurb. You could try this with some bestsellers and see what you discover.

Editors also want characters they will think about after they put the story down. This means the characters not only have to be three-dimensional, they must be dynamic, flawed in a way that makes the reader empathize with them without pity, and deeply complex. Think about Dean Koontz's *Odd Thomas*. If ever there was a reluctant hero who crossed a terrifying threshold, it's Odd. Even his name tells the reader they're about to enter a strange and dangerous place. In the YA market, we have criminal prodigy Kaz Brekkmer from *Six of Crows* by Leigh Bardugo, and Rhysand, High Lord of the Night Court from book 2 of *A Court of Thorns and Roses* by Sarah J. Maas, and one of the best villains out there is Maven Calore from *Red Queen* by Victoria Aveyard. Want to write about contemporary reality? Take a look at Star Carter from *The Hate U Give* by Angie Thomas. Star is a realistic badass who doesn't need super powers. You will fall in love with her relatable strength and humor.

Writing memorable characters isn't easy. You must work at it and work hard. It may mean rewriting some pivotal scene or dialogue or description a dozen times. So be it. You're a writer and that's your job. You wouldn't want your surgeon to practice on a single cadaver before he takes a scalpel to you. Your reader will never know the hours of rewrites that went into turning your story from a good one to one that glows, but unless you take the time and effort to deeply understand kids, what they're like, who they like, what they do and why they do it, don't send your story to an editor or agent and expect acceptance. What connects readers of any age to the characters in a YA novel is that they're all going through something difficult, some emotional, difficult inner struggle, and telling it in such a unique and engaging way the reader becomes invested in their success. It may well be caused by some outside force, some call to adventure or trial, but the struggle will be internal as well as external.

No matter what situation the protagonist faces externally, the reader can relate to that inner turmoil, fear, confusion, anxiety or indecision. That is what the reader relates to, so if you want your story to appeal to readers, agents, editors, everyone, be sure they're in the belly of the whale and know it. Teens feel strongly. Don't forget to add that depth of emotion to your protagonist, without being overly dramatic. Readers like to experience intense situations vicariously through your characters.

A glowing YA book doesn't just have teenage protagonists either. It must be so anchored in their distinct point of view that the reader believes it, no matter what age the reader might be. You have created unique characters with individual voices. The pop culture seems real, even it's pure fantasy in a made-up world. The slang, and all teens use slang, and many use foul language, must seem real too. The narrator isn't remembering what it was to be a teenager or giving the teen reader a lesson or lecture. The narrator, whether third-person or first-person protagonist's view is a teenager, viewing the world, wherever that world may be, through the eyes of youth. No adult perspectives allowed from the narrators or teen characters. The narration and/or protagonist's voice must compel the reader to identify with them immediately, to make that fast bond connection. They react to the vivid world you have created in distinct ways. Editors watch for these things. It's a fast and sure way to ascertain if the book glows.

You opened your story with a bang and grabbed your reader's attention with your fascinating but relatable character. She's received and answered the call to adventure, and she's fighting her way through hell, perhaps literally, and then what? And then, if an editor gets this far because you have nailed all the other elements to the story, you have avoided a sagging middle. You have changed locales and/or added some exciting plot twists or subplots, intriguing minor characters, or reexamined your character's goals. Hurtle crossed.

Now does the character live happily ever after? Not always. Editors know not all stories end with the characters achieving all their goals in a way they wanted or expected. This may especially be true in a series in which their struggle continues in the next book. That doesn't mean you torment the character and make him struggle through hardship and trial after trial only to lose everything and everyone he cares about in the end. After investing the emotional connection with a character, rooting for him, suffering alongside him, readers won't stand for total failure as their reward. That's no reward at all. There needs to be a sense of hope, a reason to go on fighting the good fight, believing in your dreams. There must always be the youthful exuberance for possibility, of learning enough and gaining enough experience to face another day.

This doesn't mean your story can't be dark. There are no taboo subjects in YA. Teens are experimenting with drugs, sex, and risky choices. They are exposed to world politics, stereotyping, hate, foul language, violence, bullying and crime. Reading about some of the things they are going through in a safe environment helps them feel they are not alone. Social injustice is a huge YA theme. Just don't go for trendy. Trends in YA fiction are fickle and subject to constant change. Instead, editors are looking for unique and intriguing, something that captures their attention and imagination.

Once you have it, the entire plot better move at break-neck speed. Flowery, beautiful verbiage is not the hallmark of good YA. Readers of this genre are notorious at skimming the moment they sense a section isn't vital to the plot. They're used to immediate gratification and if they can't get it from you, they will quickly go elsewhere. Editors know this. Editors do this. The moment your story sludges out backstory rather than using it sparingly to move the plot forward, you have lost their attention, and your chance at finding a publisher.

Chapter Sixteen

Writing with a Partner

Have you ever wrestled with writer's block? Sat at your computer staring at a blank page with nothing in your head but air? Ever know a reporter, personally? A reporter goes to work, sits at a desk piled with interviews to write up, events she's covered to write about, and cut-lines for photos to create. Reporters don't have time to wait for their muse to kick in. They must write, write well, and write prolifically.

That's easier said than done when the only ideas are entirely your own and you must come up with an entire novel. Did you ever feel like saying, "I lost my muse? How do I find it?" Don't panic. The whole "muse" thing is highly overrated.

The dictionary defines muse as a person or personified force who is the source of inspiration for a creative artist. Do you really have to have that to write? Do you think you need to be inspired or is that story that's lost in your head only just out of reach? You don't need some intangible force to help you. What you really need is some quiet time to float. Unlike muses, floating is highly underrated.

There are different kinds of floating. You can climb on a raft and float down a river or just get on a tube and float in your pool. Or, you can fill your bathtub with hot water, lay back, close your eyes, and float. Of course, what floating really means is dissociating yourself. No matter how you do it, through real floating, laying in a green field, smelling the roses, sitting back in a lounge chair and closing your eyes, going into a dark room and meditating or sitting in your office chair with your eyes closed for ten minutes, floating helps you find that inner spot where your stories are hiding. Some writers run so they can kick off endorphins and when in the "zone" they float. Whatever way works for you, do it. If you shut off the constant inner voice yammering inside your head, the ideas will flow. So, float.

This will usually kickstart your creative juices, but we understand that sometimes despite all your best effort, you lack motivation. Sometimes the prose doesn't flow, which is why events like National Novel Writing Month (https://nanowrimo.org) exist. In November, you sit down with a nation of writers there to support you, hold you accountable and share in your experience. They force you to just get it down on paper, to write an entire novel in a single month. That doesn't consider the months of edits ahead of you, but it forces you to write something, every single day.

What if it's not November and you've floated until your skin prunes and your brain feels like lead, or like it's full of cotton and there's nothing in there, no ideas, no words, nada? In other words, the dreaded writer's block has landed. Most writers deal with this problem at one time or another. Sometimes the answer to that problem can be a writing partner, rather than thousands of random strangers.

Even if you don't have writer's block, or an empty head, there are times in your writing where you could use a fresh eye, a new view point, a partner with different experiences to draw from. Especially when writing for young adults, having a friend, a fellow writer, or children of your own is important. This can't be repeated enough; you have to know teens. You need to understand your audience. Merely reading bundles of young adult or middle grade books is not enough. If that means finding a writing partner to help, do it, try it on, see how it fits.

One famous writing pair is Douglas Preston and Lincoln Child. These two have penned best seller after best seller. Lincoln Child wrote a long article on the process he and Preston went through to tone and perfect their partnership. Child said, "Our collaborative process has changed significantly in the twenty-five—alas, yes, twenty-five—years since we started writing novels together. Initially, Doug (who at the time had more experience writing professionally, albeit nonfiction) wrote the first drafts of the majority of the chapters. I (as a former trade editor at a New York publishing house who spent a great deal of time not only editing manuscripts but at times suggesting wholesale revisions to the underlying plots) wrote up the initial chapter outlines, and then rewrote Doug's drafts."

Preston was a world traveler who Child said could write creditably about almost any location while Child was a systems analyst. Their different backgrounds gave them a wider range of experiences to draw from, which can make a book much more detailed and more fun to read.

Child says, "While we continue to develop chapter outlines jointly, brainstorm what direction a novel should take, and revise one another's prose, we each tend to "champion" (for want of a better term) certain books. This entails writing the lion's share of a particular story and taking the lead on its development—again, always in frequent consultation with our writing partner."

There are some real things to think about when writing in a genre containing characters with which you are not familiar. Say you have a contract to write four chick lit books about women and the men they meet in the city. There you are, fiftyish, living in the country with your dogs, no friends in the thirty-something world, living the modern dating scene. Or maybe that's the kind of book you want to write because it's what you read. However, you don't have any ideas about characters. Enter that friend you met in creative writing in college. She now lives in New York and is working in the restaurant world. Time to reconnect. She knows the people and the world. You went on and became a writer. Together, you have all the right stuff to create a great chick lit book.

Now imagine you're in the same situation. You've published chick lit for five years but you're tired of it. Young Adult is hot. You have grandkids or nieces and nephews in the right age group, but essentially you need to know more about kids; what they do, what they like, how they behave in school. It's time to find a friend who teaches in high school, or you need to volunteer at the Y, at a high school, and learn the hard way. A co-writer who already knows kids is really the perfect answer. That person can give you plot ideas, help you create believable characters, and when you get stuck, can help you out.

Writing with a partner is usually better with someone you know well, so maybe there's a member of your family who has the right position to join you and collaborate on a project. Mother-daughter teams exist just like mother-son teams. When Kathy Reichs, author of the *Temperance Brennan* series which was turned into the hit TV show *Bones,* decided to branch out into YA stories, she turned to her son Brendan for help. Balancing work with family can be tough, especially when the two overlap. To keep things operating smoothly, Brendan calls his co-writer "Kathy" when discussing work issues and "Mom," when they're off the clock.

Father-son teams are out there as well. Dick Francis was the Queen of England's steeplechase jockey. He was on the NY Times best seller list for a long time. He penned several novels with his son, Felix, before he passed away. Now Felix Francis is an author. Maybe the help you need is in the family.

Ten Reasons to Write with a Partner

1.   Collaborating makes you a better writer (and maybe a better person).

Most teams will tell you working together has made them better people. Less ego-involved and controlling. More open and trusting. The long-term effect of writing with someone else is far more profound than expected. It's humanizing. You learn to accept and welcome your differences and most of your idiosyncrasies.

The rewards of collaboration often transcend success. Many writers find success on their own, but it isn't until they wrote with a partner they found real fulfillment.

"What we do together has been not just professionally but personally very nourishing," script-writer Lowell Ganz says about his long, luminous career with Babaloo Mandel (*City Slickers; Parenthood*), "to have done it with, and to still be doing it, together."

2.   It's a dog-eat-dog business - and vice versa - but when you write with a partner, there's always one person in town looking out for your interests.

As you well know, the misery curve for all writers is legendary. Conventional wisdom says it takes five to ten years to learn the craft of writing, and five books before you finally sell one. There are exceptions, of course, keeping hope alive, but with the advent of e-books, the competition just gets harder, the profits from being a writer smaller. When you write with a partner, there is at least one person you can talk to who knows your pain, who backs you up, who says, "Hey, we'll make it." That one person might be all you need to remain sane.

It may be a cold world out there for writers, but one of the best ways to stay warm is with a writing partner, collaborating.

3.   Writing is lonely. It doesn't have to be (and it isn't if you write with a partner).

Sitting at your desk, writing all alone, can be so depressing. It can also be engrossing and uplifting, but it's a lonely job. When you write with a partner, you can always find someone interested in listening, offering constructive comments and providing you with a reason to go out for coffee or a glass of wine. Many books have been plotted and critiqued and edited at Starbucks®.

4.   Two imaginations really are better than one.

If you're a writer, you all know that trapped, helpless feeling. Your story gets stuck in the corner. You think, "No escape." But if you write with a partner, you help each other figure it out and find your way out of the confusion. Part of writing great books comes from putting the characters into horrible problems and then getting them out. What if you wrote your character into a corner and you can't think of a single way to get them out. The solution is calling your partner. Two imaginations, one with a different scope of experiences added to yours, will find a way to solve the problem. It's like *MacGyver* writing. You need MacGyver's knowledge and imagination to get your character out of the spot you stuck him in. This can be especially true in YA fiction. After all, teenagers are known for getting themselves into trouble and for trying new things.

Having a partner when you're trying to think of that high-concept idea that's going to make you famous can really add height to your ideas. Your partner may have that one idea, or twist on an idea you've been simmering, inside his or her head. When writing YA, you need someone who is around teens all the time. It will give you the edge on other writers by adding a dose of realism to the mix. Your partner might be good at thinking of subjects that will interest them. Most fifteen-year-olds are interested in their phone. The character in *Jumanji: Welcome to the Jungle,* Bethany, first thing she does when she's dropped into the world of Jumanji is hunt for her phone, so she can post the experience on Instagram. A more typical reaction could not be found. However, teens have got to be interested in more than their phones. Right? So, if you're going to write YA, you at least need to know teenagers, or someone who does know them.

There is another important issue to examine when you're thinking about needing a partner. If you have a strong protagonist who is a guy and you're not a male, getting input from a guy is extremely helpful. A partner who is the opposite sex can help with guy-speak, or girl-speak, you know, dude language, as well as how males, boys, in general think. Believe it or not, the male perspective is different from the female one.

5.   Collaboration leads to better brainstorming.

We're all told to be bold (there's magic in it,) but being bold while brainstorming is easier when you write with a partner. Why? Instant feedback. When you write alone, you're your own worst critic. You question your work; the backspace key has a hole worn into it. But a co-writer can see the potential in ideas you might otherwise throw away. Positive feedback from someone who's opinions you value energizes and encourages experimentation. Defeats defeatism. Promotes enthusiasm. But all the enthusiasm in the world is no substitute for actually doing the writing. Developing productive work habits. And having a partner helps here, too. A writing workout partner...because when you have someone writing more than you, you feel guilty. When there's someone waiting for you to produce pages, you work.

6. A writing workout partner helps you stay focused and productive.

You must work because your partner is working. If you feel like you'd rather go to the beach and you know your writing partner is at home going over the last pages you produced and is expecting more, you don't go to the beach. You stay home and work. When one of the team members get tired or discouraged, the other one can take over and keep things going.

Partners also bring different work habits to the collaboration, and they often improve over time. If one of the team members is a hard charger, nose-to-the-grindstone kind of writer, the other team member will feel the pressure and step up, often becoming a better writer, better organized and better at self-motivation.

7. Complementing (and complimenting) each other leads to stronger books.

Having lots in common helps a writing team stay together and on the same page, but their differences - the creative yin-yang - are just as important. It is this combination, this complementarity that gives each collaboration its unique richness and range of experience, knowledge, and talent to tap. That's why it's important to find a partner who has skills you don't possess. If you write YA fiction, the best partner would be one who lives in that world, has knowledge of teenagers, what they like, what they're like. And maybe, another great addition to your team would be a couple of teenagers to use as beta readers. Get your feedback straight from the horse's mouth.

8.   Writing with a partner improves mental health (and it's cheaper than antidepressants).

It's no wonder we've all got therapists and gurus on speed dial. Anxiety is so rampant in writers (especially women, but men suffer, too) that a recent conference sponsored by the Institute for Psychoanalytic Training and Research was devoted to finding ways to assuage it. One of the strategies that the conference predicted would be most successful was an effective creativity support group. And that support group can be your writing partner. It takes the terror out of being in the room alone with that blank sheet of paper staring at you from the computer screen with not one word on it. That terror is all too common. Having someone help you formulate those first words, push you on with support and encouraging words, helps.

10.   A partner can help you conquer writer's block.

When you reach a spot in your book and your mind goes blank, what do you do? If you have a partner, there is someone else out there who knows your story, who's as deeply involved as you are. Together, you can figure out where to go next, what steps your characters need to take to make the story work. There are just some places in books, where even if you have a detailed outline, there's a hole. "How do I get from here to there?" Then there's the *MacGyver* aspect. "Think of a way to get me out of this nightmare because I'm stuck." A partner can talk you off the ledge. "It's okay, here's an idea. What do you think?"

11.   Discuss your expectations for each other in the writing process.

Before you fully commit to a writing partnership, have an in-depth discussion with your prospective partner on your writing process and goals. Do this even if your partner is your spouse, best friend, or sibling. By making sure you're as on the same page as possible up front, you can avoid a great deal of grief down the road.

Sometimes it's not all light and roses. Sometimes things can go south.

What if you were working on a project and your partner flaked? What if you were producing a show with two guys and then you stopped getting along? You write a story with a friend and you want to keep pursuing it and she doesn't. Sometimes things just don't work out. That can happen with or without a partner. You can suddenly decide, in the middle of a project, it's not good, you're wasting your time, file it. Writing with a partner is no different. Not everything in life is a breeze. Not everything goes as planned. But if you're tossing around the idea of writing with a partner, try it. Can't hurt, right?

Even if it doesn't work out for you. Even if you think you could never work with someone else or don't like sharing, if you want to write something big, with aspects or elements you know nothing about, and you have a friend who can collaborate with you and wants to take on the project; consider it. Writing with a partner can take some of the load off your shoulders. Input from a different viewpoint can make your work more interesting and better. And who doesn't want that?

Here are some famous writing duos you may or may not have heard about.

J.R.R. Tolkien and C.S. Lewis

Not all writing pairs write the same stories at the same time. Tolkien and Lewis, unarguably two of the greatest fantasy writers who ever lived, never credited each other on their books, but they mailed their work back and forth to each other constantly, forever revising each other's work to make it just perfect. They even debated one of Tolkien's poems for over 30 years! That's devotion.

H.P. Lovecraft and Harry Houdini

In the 1920s, Houdini was the world's greatest escape artist magician. Lovecraft wrote stories about old gods and tentacled horrors from dimensions unknown to man. Their collaboration resulted in the short-story _Imprisoned with the Pharaohs_, which is, of course, a first person account of the time Houdini escaped from a pyramid and was nearly eaten by the ancient god who inspired the sphinx. Most of the time you might say this story probably isn't 100% true, but this _was_ Harry Houdini...

Kami Garcia and Margaret Stohl

Garcia and Stohl were already friends when Stohl's kids dared the two to write a book together. What began as a lark turned into the _Beautiful Creatures_ franchise. Five books, a movie, and several short stories later, they've clearly proven how well they work together. Even better, they're still friends!

Matt Stone and Trey Parker

What started as two college buddies trying to crack each other up became the comedy genius behind _South Park, BASEketball, The Book of Mormon_, and others. Stone and Parker are reportedly extremely vigilant about keeping outsiders from getting between them, which is no mean feat when you've been one of the most successful writing teams in the world for over a decade.

Stephen King and Tabitha King

Stephen and Tabitha are a literary power couple with a literary power family. The King family is bursting at the seams with successful writers; both of their sons have also published books. The Kings have been married since 1971, and both have published multiple novels. Although Stephen King's reputation and output has far exceeded his wife's, her nine novels have also been well-received. Tabitha has played the often unsung but invaluable role of the supportive spouse. When Stephen first began writing his breakout hit *Carrie*, he felt he couldn't write convincingly from a girl's perspective and threw out the first pages he'd drafted. Tabitha urged him to keep trying, aiding him throughout the process of getting inside the mind of a woman. Without her insight, Stephen's glorious career as a horror writer might never have taken off.

Chapter Seventeen

Marketing Your Book Before and After Publication

Before

There are so many ways to get published. Everyone's journey to get there is different and begins with that first step. The first step for most is writing a book. So, you write the longest, biggest, YA urban fantasy ever written. It has everything in it but the kitchen sink. You printed it out and you're holding in your hands this magnificent manuscript. Now what do you do?

One of the best ways to find out what to do is to join a local writer's group. There are many across the country. Most have monthly meetings you can attend, meet new people, and learn how to get that fantastic manuscript published.

Writers groups are a wonderful way to improve your writing skills, find a critique group, network with other writers, and get help building your writer's resume. The big ones, Romance Writers of America, Science Fiction and Fantasy Writers of America, and Mystery Writers of America have subgroups that support Middle Grade and Young Adult writers of those genres. They also have state and local groups where you can attend monthly meetings and conferences and find critique partners. Do an online search and you will be shocked at how many varieties of writing groups there are just in your home state, quite possibly in your home town.

Don't have time to attend a location meeting? There are a lot of groups you can join online and share your work for feedback or even just lurk and browse for tips and information, such as The Hatrack River Writers Group, The Reddit Writers Group, The Next Big Writer, NANOWRIMO (National Novel Writing Month) and Insecure Writers Support Group. Within these and many other forums you can find support, encouragement, critiques, beta readers, reviews, information and resources. Writing doesn't need to be lonely all the time.

Learning to like networking? Attend conferences. They happen in every state. Some are affiliated with writing associations and some are promoted by libraries and other reader and writer's groups. The New York Pitch Conference draws hundreds of writers, agents and editors every year. There are websites online that list every important book conference, book fair and fests happening throughout the year. Most of these conferences will have workshops. Some, like the Romance Writers of America's national conference, will feature well over fifty workshops presenting everything from how to write a query letter, how to format your submission, how to write a good pitch, all the way to how people dressed in the middle ages, complete with a fashion show that includes undergarments.

Every time you attend one of these conferences you will have various opportunities to advance your knowledge and your writing career. You'll learn more about writing and the publishing industry, perhaps have the opportunity to pitch your book to an agent or editor. Check this box on your resume. Agents and editors appreciate knowing you're working on becoming a better writer. One of the agents you meet might even give you their card and invite you to submit your work.

Joining professional writing organizations and attending conferences looks great on your writer's resume. The camaraderie, networking time, and fun you have at these conferences can't be downplayed either. You'll meet readers, authors, agents, publishers, people who may be able to help you on your journey to getting published.

The best advice is writing every day. Hone your skills, learn to take criticism, a very important lesson, learn to write tightly and edit your work. Editors, agents and publishers don't have the time to wade through a manuscript filled with grammatical errors and sloppy writing. You need to learn to write well and polish your work. Learn to create your muse not wait for its arrival. Deadlines are unforgiving in any publishing world. Learn to take constructive, destructive and any kind of criticism. Critique group members might know what they're talking about. When they hand you back a chapter with red and green and blue ink all over it, be happy. Thank them, whether you decide to take their advice or not. Someone is trying to help you. Someone took the time to read your work and explain to you how to make it better. Online critique partners can be just as hard. Learn to use the input positively, take it like a professional, and improve your writing.

Writing is a skill. To get a job using that skill, you need to create a resume just as you would if you were applying for any job. Let's review that again: join a writing group, a critique group, attend conferences, learn and improve your craft.

Build your resume. You can build it by entering contests. Writing and literature organizations sponsor lots of them for published authors, and the Romance Writers of America and its affiliate chapters sponsor a lot of contests for unpublished writers. There are probably many contests for unpublished authors. Do an internet search. A win is a chalk mark on your resume.

Volunteer for your local writers' group. Write for its newsletter. Editors are always scrambling for material. A published article, even if it's in your group's newsletter, is a published article.

Here's a sneaky way to get publishing credits. Not many people know about this. Newspapers, both online and printed publications, are also always searching for material and open to submissions. Newspaper editors and editors of online publications rarely turn away material. If you belong to a group like Rotary or the Elks Club, attend meetings, take notes, write them up and send them into the local newspaper. Every time you write about the Little League game you went to, your kid's soccer team's big win, or the bake sale held by the PTA and send it to the newspaper, it has a huge chance of making it into the paper. You won't get paid, but now you have legitimate writing credits. Make sure you ask for a byline. They will usually be glad to give it to you. Take photos and send them with the article and you can get your kid's picture in the paper as a bonus.

These are many ways to build your writer's resume. When you write a fiction book about a little boy who grew up in Norway, having credentials to back up that writing can help. It adds to your resume. Maybe you grew up in Norway. Add that to your resume. If you're writing a book about cowboys, it helps to know horses, own cows, live on a ranch, or be married to one (a cowboy not a cow). It can get that book looked at where it might otherwise be ignored. If you're a teacher, write young adult books and submit them with a query letter touting your years dealing with teens. You have another credential for your resume.

After

So, you received plenty of good advice and help and critiques and got your book published or you self-published and now you think wow, the hard work is done. Guess again. The work is just beginning. Marketing after publication has become the job of the writer in almost every instance. If you read any book on marketing, it will tell you to work on developing your online presence and spreading word about the upcoming release of your novel. This is all well and good, and you should spend some time on this, but you won't see much of a payoff from it. So, what do you do? You would think that when you write a book that's the time to get creative, but it's not. The time is now! Your books will not sell themselves and most publishers don't have the funds for marketing books by unknown authors. To say you're not good at it, or you tried (a little without much consistency) and then stopped, is not going to work. The characters in the chapter pic don't look uncomfortable in their roles for no reason. Everyone understands. You just want to write. Who doesn't? But this is a business, and if you want to be a professional writer, you have to act like one.

You will have to do a lot of work to get your book some attention. Selling your product, which is your book, works best when there is a face-to-face interaction between the buyer and the seller. Most authors do book signings and speak at schools and libraries. This is a good way to sell your book, but it cannot be the only way you personally market to potential buyers. Think of rappers like 50 Cent, Dr. Dre or Lil Wayne talking about how they used to sell copies of their CD's out of the trunk of their car. This needs to be you. Think of yourself as a musician that is trying relentlessly to get heard. If you've ever been to Nashville, you go downtown and there are musicians on the corner singing everywhere, and they are there every night just to be heard. The days of door-to-door salesmen are over, so don't go knocking on any unsafe doors, but there are many other ways to get around and meet prospective buyers.

One good way is to work a job where you meet a lot of people— which doesn't mean quit a lucrative job and take a job parking cars, so you can talk to people as they hand you their keys. But if you have a job where you meet other people, or even if you have a lot of coworkers, you can market your books. You could market your books while working as a server in restaurants, driving for a ride-sharing service and a good one for YA writers is working as a teacher or substitute teacher. If you're a good writer, then it is plausible to assume you went to college. Subbing is hard work but having a book and some bookmarks to give away will make the job more rewarding and easier. People get excited when they meet a published author. They will ask you if you're famous or say that they've heard of your book when they haven't. You can give away a book to one student every time you sub, and always write inside the cover asking them to write a line about what they think of it on Amazon® or Goodreads.

Depending on the genre of your book, you might want to market to different grades. If you write YA novels, hit the middle and high schools. Share information with the staff in the teachers' lounge. Leave them bookmarkers. Talk to the librarians and see if they will order some. Teachers may request classroom sets. Even if you don't work as a sub, you can network your local districts, find out who orders the books for their libraries, give them some free samples and ask them to order it for their district.

Driving for Uber is another interesting way to connect to people. Riders get excited to be taking a ride from a published author. ALWAYS carry business cards and/or bookmarks. You get a lot of trips to the airport and these people always have time on their hands to read a good novel that you recommended to them. If you ride in an uber, leave a bookmark on the seat for the next patron.

Marketing your book as a server takes being able to talk to and connect to people. Waiting tables is tough, but it does provide opportunities to chitchat with people as they eat, and you can leave a bookmark in with the check. If you eat out, leave the waitress a bookmark with her tip (make sure it's a good one!).

Doing readings at your local library is a good way to get your book some attention. The library might advertise that you will be speaking there, and people and kids show up to hear you read an excerpt from your book. If your book isn't in the library, you can speak to the librarian and go to the library's website where you can try to get your book in their system. You can also give a few copies to the librarian, say you're a local published author, and they will add your book. Many have local author sections in their libraries.

Another way to market your book without meeting people face-to-face is to leave rack cards. What are rack cards? They're those cards you see in racks, like at businesses, or even the grocery stores. Lots of stores have sections where you first walk in where there are real estate flyers, daily special flyers and racks of "free" ads, including a snazzy rack card with a picture of your book cover on it, a short blurb about the book and where people can find it and on the back side a short bio, perhaps with your picture and the fact that you're a local author. Hotel lobbies are another great place to find card racks. They have racks with touristy maps or postcards, or flyers about local events and sites. Why not a card of a local author with a great book? Hotel guests often like to read at night, and why not download your book to their iPad or phone and read it on the plane trip home, too? Stores will often put these out for you, too. Never be afraid to ask. All they can do is say no.

A really good way to meet people who will buy your book in person is by going to writing conferences. This is also a good way to hone your writing skills. Contact the company putting on the conference and hopefully it can get you a table where you can do signings. This might cost some money, but it's worth it for the exposure you get to readers. You may also have to do some traveling. New York has great conferences, and that's where all the big publishers are. Hopefully you made Facebook and Amazon author pages. These aren't the best ways to get sales, but they are a necessity. The key to getting likes for your Facebook page is by joining groups. There are Facebook groups where the members will like your page if you like theirs. Search like for like. This is also the same way to get followers on Twitter and Instagram. You can search follow for follow and get the same results or find lists with people who will follow you back. This might not sell your book, but it's a way to give yourself credibility.

A way to get your book noticed is to win writing contests. Enter your book in any contest that you can. Winning a writing contest will bring a lot of positive attention to your book. Some contests offer to publicize your book as part of the entry. It also helps to have a lot of reviews for your book. If you give away books, ask the person for a short review on Amazon or Goodreads. Make sure you hit up relatives and friends for some blurbs or reviews. You can also ask your editor to do one.

More and more people are buying everything online, but at the same time there are more and more books being added online. Because of KDP/CreateSpace from Amazon, anyone can get a book published and this has overloaded the market, and not in a good way. There is a ton of material out there. Seriously, have you ever purchased a book that was marketed to you on Facebook or Twitter? And you see people pushing their books every time you log in. Get out and sell. Use meeting people at work to tell them how amazing your book is. Hand out bookmarks and business cards to everyone. If your book is good enough, then you should invest in it. Take the profits from your books and buy books with the money. Get out there. Stop reading and go, now.

Unless you signed a contract with one of the "Big 5," and even if you did and they don't consider you to be their next Stephen King, selling yourself and your book is on you as the author. You might get some help from smaller publishers, but the heavy-lifting is on the author. And if you self-pubbed, it's all on you. There is one self-published author out there who made it to the NY Times best seller list in a very slick way. He's rich, so he bought a lot, and I mean a lot, of his books. Instant best seller. If you're not rich, you better learn how to promote yourself. Since many writers are introverts, this could be difficult.

The Big 5 is the nickname for the major trade book publishing companies. Four are in the United States. Getting published by one of the Big 5 book publishers is the goal of many authors, as being published by a major publishing house is perceived to have some advantages over smaller presses or self-publishing. Those advantages are mostly in the amount of dollars the big houses are willing to spend promoting their authors.

Formerly known as "The Big 6" (until Random House and Penguin officially merged in June 2013), all the publishers have headquarters in the hub of book publishing, New York City.

Hachette Book Group

Hachette Book Group (HBG) is a division of the second-largest trade and educational book publisher in the world, Hachette Livre. Hachette Livre is based in France and is a subsidiary of the French media company, Lagardère. Hachette's publishing divisions include Grand Central Publishing; Little, Brown and Company; Little, Brown and Company Books for Young Readers; Faith Words; Center Street; Orbit; Yen Press; Hachette Audio; and Hachette Digital. Read about Forever, Hachette's Romance line, and about Forever Yours, its digital-first Romance line.

HarperCollins

HarperCollins Publishers is a subsidiary of News Corp, the global media company led by Rupert Murdoch. Some of HarperCollins publishers and imprints are HarperCollins; William Morrow; Avon Books; Broadside Books; Harper Business; HarperCollins Childrens; HarperTeen; Ecco Books; It Books; Newmarket Press; Harper One; Harper Voyager US; Harper Perennial; HarperAcademic and Harper Audio.

Macmillan Publishers

Macmillan is a global trade publishing company, which is owned by the German Company Verlagsgruppe Georg von Holtzbrinck, with imprints in the United States, Germany, the United Kingdom, Australia, South Africa, and around the world.

The Macmillan U.S. trade book publishers include Farrar, Straus and Giroux; Henry Holt and Company; Picador; St. Martin's Press; Tor/Forge; Macmillan Audio; and Macmillan Children's Publishing Group. Macmillan also publishes into the college and academic book marketplace.

Penguin Random House

Originally international publishing giants in their own rights, on July 1, 2013, Penguin, a Pearson company, and Random House, owned by the German company Bertelsmann, combined their adult and children's fiction and nonfiction print and digital trade book publishing divisions.

As a result, Penguin Random House has nearly 250 imprints and publishing houses. Some of the most well-known Penguin Random House publishing groups are Random House Publishing Group, Knopf Doubleday Publishing Group; Crown Publishing Group; Penguin Group U.S.; Dorling Kindersley; Mass Market Paperbacks, Penguin Group U.S.; Random House Children's Books; Penguin Young Readers Group, U.S.

Simon & Schuster

Simon & Schuster was founded in 1924 by Richard L. (Dick) Simon and M. Lincoln (Max) Schuster with a bestselling crossword puzzle book. At various times in its history, it has been owned by Marshall Field, Gulf + Western, and Viacom. Simon and Schuster is currently the publishing arm of the media company CBS Corporation, where its diverse offerings include books in the adult publishing, children's publishing, audiobooks and digital book arenas.

Simon & Schuster's publishing divisions and imprints include Atria, Folger Shakespeare Library, Free Press, Gallery Books, Howard Books, Pocket Books, Scribner, Simon & Schuster, Threshold Editions, and Touchstone.

So, there they are, the ideal, the pinnacle of every author's hopes are to get published by one of these companies. Well, you better get an agent because they don't take submissions from ordinary folks. All their submissions are sent to them by agents. Authors who don't have agents, can self-pub or search for one of the many smaller publishing firms to work with.

Small Presses

Being published by a small press isn't an insult. They are hard sells too, and even have some advantages over the Big 5. In fact, they don't have to publish just high concept books and will publish those mid-listers the big houses no longer want. They also now own the largest share of the book market, which means they are publishing more books than the Big 5.

First, do your homework. See how long they have been in business. Small presses fold at an alarming rate, for various reasons. Check out their websites. Are they professional? Do they have regular new releases? Do they have a lot of books under their belt? What do they publish? Are their covers professional? Go to Amazon and look inside some of their books. Are they well edited and formatted professionally? If so, find out how/when and if they are currently taking submissions and what they are looking for.

Even though they are a small press, if they are traditional publishers (not vanity presses that charge you to publish your work), you must still submit and hook their interest before they even consider you. You must hone your writing skills until you can do that.

Self-Promotion

When you do get published, you better have some ideas about how to promote yourself and your work. There is a lot of current controversy about the Big 5 turning some of their traditional imprints into digital-only imprints and offering contracts to new and already-published authors. Some of the more elitist writing organizations won't accept authors from these lines into their ranks. Who knows whether this is an attempt to save money or to offset the recent flood of self-published work hitting the digital market, but it is a big change. Some authors are happy to sign with one of these companies no matter what the fine print says, others are choosing to say no, , actually turning down an offer of publication, to go with self-publishing or a small press company.

Two authors, Barry Eisler and Matthew Reilly decided to self-pub after being published through a large publisher with an agent. They made this choice because agents take a portion of your royalties, and they felt they could make it on their own. They were right. So, it can be done. Eisler had a name before he went out on his own and that helped. Reilly made it on the back of his writing skills and had a great promo plan.

Here is a plan for promoting your book and yourself.

If you don't have time to do all of these things, at least do some of them.

Start Promoting Yourself Early

The most powerful and essential steps you can take toward promoting your book begin long before the actual writing of the book. Three years before the book is published--if you can--start building a network of supporters and reviewers. Keep track of everyone you meet as you research and write the book. Pay special attention to, and make notes about, those who demonstrate a genuine enthusiasm for you and your project. As the project evolves, keep in touch with these people. You might send them an occasional email or keep in touch via a social networking site like LinkedIn or Facebook.

Contribute to Web Forums

Every field has at least one or two forums that people interested in your subject know and read. Some were noted earlier. Find and join these forums. Contribute to them freely. Give advice and reach out. Offer to help others. Put a link to your blog or website in your signature line. When you have a book contract and/or a book title, add the title to your signature line.

Start a Blog

Early in the process of researching and thinking about your book, start a blog. Add 120-130 words each day of helpful, inspirational information on issues in your field, which are related to the subjects in your book. Aim to create a genuinely useful body of knowledge over the following 12 months.

Write a Remarkable Book

Set out to write a remarkable book. If your book is not remarkable, keep working on it until it is. Don't stop until your reviewers start saying things like, "I loved it! This book is amazing!" A remarkable book will generate word-of-mouth publicity. One person will read it and recommend it to his or her friends. They will recommend it to their friends. This is the best publicity you can get.

Cultivate a Positive Attitude about Book Promotion

Think of book promotion as storytelling. The story you are telling is why you wrote your book, how it can help others, and how the world will benefit from your book. If you can develop a positive attitude about book promotion, people will pick up on it and tune in immediately. Some writers resent the chore of marketing. Their attitude seems to be, "I'm a writer. Marketing is the publisher's job. Promoting my own book shouldn't be my responsibility." Unfortunately--unless you're Stephen King or J.K. Rowling, the publisher probably won't have the budget to market your book. If you don't promote your book, no one else will.

Create a Brand

Who do you want the world of book readers to think you are? What do you mostly write? Why is your work important, different, and better than others? What do you like to read? Think about this carefully. You need to package "yourself" and your book(s) in a catchy, positive way. If you don't create a brand, readers will create one for you, and it may not be the one you want. Everyone is judged, evaluated and categorized. Make sure you're in the category you choose yourself.

Do you need a logo? Maybe. It depends on if you write some high-concept or unique stories. It can be as simple as what font you always use on your promo banners and website headers to an actual symbol. It can also be defined by certain color choices you always use. Be careful not to get too bogged down in genre images or moods unless that is the only thing you write, and you want readers to immediately identify you by that.

You do need a tag line (a concise mission statement) added to your author name, and you need to consider whether you want to write under your own name or use a pseudonym (especially if you write in different genres). This will define you and help you stand out from the crowd. It will help readers identify you and your work and get their attention.

The key to branding is consistency. Use the same "branding" on all your banners, headers and promotional material. Use the same colors, logos, fonts, on every social media platform. This will help readers instantly "recognize" you and your work.

Create a Media Kit

Your media kit should include:

- Professionally printed business cards with the book cover on one side and your contact information on the other side. Do not try to print them on your home printer. This is a time to invest in your product and yourself, not save money.

- A head shot by a professional photographer or a talented amateur. It should be well lit, with a neutral background. Your eyes should sparkle.

- A 100 – 150-word biography. The main purpose of the biography is to tell a reader why you are uniquely qualified to have written this particular book.

- A 'one-sheet' for the book: a single piece of paper with a glossy print of the book cover on one side and a one-page description of the book on the other side. Be sure to include a few short blurbs and recommendations from colleagues and friends in the description.

Create a Book Pitch

Consider writing at least three sales pitches for your book: 10 seconds, 30 seconds, and 60 seconds. When someone asks what the book is about, give them the 10 second pitch. If the person responds with interest, have a longer pitch ready. Practice your pitches on friends until they tell you the pitches work.

Build a Website

As publication day approaches, build a full website. Be sure it promotes your brand as well as your body of work. The website should include:

- A book blog, in which you write updates, corrections, errata and respond to reader comments and suggestions. This book blog may become the basis for the second edition of your book.
- Samples from your book, even your work in progress.
- A link to the Amazon and publisher's page for your book, so people can buy the book online.
- Your media kit.
- Book reviews and blurbs.
- Your schedule of appearances, including bookstores, speaking engagements and conferences.
- Contact information.

Get Book Reviews from Individuals

Six months (nine if possible) before the book is due to appear in book stores, start asking people for reviews and blurbs. Send reviewers a printed galley proof of your book. If you don't yet have printed galley proofs, send a PDF containing the first two chapters, a table of contents and your bio.

Don't be afraid to approach the 'biggest names' in your field. (This is important.) Ask for both reviews and blurbs. Busy people may only have time to write a few sentences.

Virtual Book Tours

There are dozens of online book tour companies that offer a variety of different services. They are happy to use your branding materials in their promotional packages. They can schedule cover reveals, media blasts like thunderclaps (hundreds or thousands of participants retweet, like or repost your PR), book reviews and excerpts, author interviews, and more. Anything you do to get your book in front of readers is a good thing. Do your research and find a company that has a lot of followers on its social media platforms and a good reputation with past author tours and one that specializes in your genre.

Write Articles

Every field has e-zines, websites and magazines that advocate or deal with the subject of your book. Find them. Once you know where they are, look through them and figure out which ones talk to the audience for your book. Contact those sites or publications and pitch articles that will be of interest to their readers.

Schedule articles to appear around the time your book will appear in bookstores and on Amazon. For example, if your book is going to appear in bookstores and on Amazon in mid-June, schedule your articles to appear in July, August, and September.

Remember to pitch articles early, because many magazines and e-zines have a 3-6-month lead time. Mention your book title somewhere in the article. In online articles, link the book title to its Amazon page so readers can click over and buy the book.

Get Book Reviews from e-zines and Magazines

Ask websites, e-zines and magazines in your field to review your book. Some websites or e-zines may offer to trade, to review your book if you write an article for them.

Get 20 Amazon Reviews

Amazon reviews are amazingly effective. Everyone from book buyers to publishers read them. Your goal is to get at least 20 reviews. Contact everyone you know and ask each of them if they would give your book an honest review. Let them know it can be brief. If they agree, send them either a galley proof, a promotional copy of the book, or a PDF containing a table of contents, two sample chapters, and your bio.

Amazon's Top Customer Reviewers are another source of high-value reviews. Find the reviewers who deal with books in your area. Write to them. Tell them you have written a book they might be interested in, and that you'd appreciate a review. If they respond, send them a galley proof or a promotional copy of your book. You can get free copies of your book using Prolific Works (previously Instafreebie), an online marketing company that provides its readers with free new reads or other similar services. Its readers are encouraged to write reviews, too. What is most useful to you is that you can opt out of their giveaways if you like, and you can use a code for your choice of reviewers to download a free copy of your book in either pdf, Kindle®, or NOOK®. The files are encrypted, so you don't need to worry that anyone will steal your work or that it will be handed out to everyone for free.

Get Mentioned in email Blasts

Look for organizations in your field that send large-volume emails. Try to get your book reviewed in their emails or newsletters. When the number of people receiving the emails is 100,000 or more it's sometimes referred to as an email blast. There are plenty of companies that will do this for a fee.

Speak at Conferences

As a published author, you have the qualifications necessary to speak at conferences. Contact conference organizers at least six months in advance. At first you may have to register and pay a fee to speak. Later, when you become better known, conferences may seek you out, and may even pay you to speak.

You should be prepared to give a 45-minute presentation. A useful way to structure a 45-minute presentation is to speak for 30 minutes and take questions from the floor for the last 15 minutes. Plan to take a few minutes after your speech to circulate with the audience. Have a table in the back of the room where you or someone on your team sells books.

Social Media

This can be a time suck, so develop a plan and try to stick to it. Many authors do quick, live chat on Facebook or other social media. People like to interact on social media, especially kids and they're your market so seek them out where they hang. Kids love variety. They use Twitter, Facebook, Instagram, Snapchat and WhatsApp. It may seem complicated, but all you need to learn are the basics. A quick reading, a promo or contest, are all good way to garner more followers to your site or readers to your books. Who doesn't like a free book or gift certificate? If you do this on a regular basis, you get to "know" your fans.

Teens use free text messaging apps like Kik Messenger or GroupMe, so parents don't see the messages in their text feeds, and don't get charged for them. They use apps like Tik Tok, including musical.ly to share karaoke or other music videos. They use meet and dating apps, and even some destructive confessional apps like Whisper.

It's unlikely that you could or would want to keep up on the newest apps, and even if you thought you were hitting the trendiest apps, kids would begin using something else. Just use the ones you can figure out and enjoy using. Whichever platforms you use, appeal to your target audience and use your branding.

On Facebook, you can call out their names and welcome them as you see them log into your chat. This is how you develop personal relationships with fans, who once devoted will read everything you write and tell everyone they know about you on social media, review sites, and more. You can create a "street team" of PR enthusiasts.

Some authors have their own reading groups, on Facebook, Goodreads and other forums. They may only read and review your books or may read and review other books in that genre too, but if you interact with them, throw them out some free bling once in a while, they will be enthusiastic about you as a writer. If they "like" you, they will follow you and shout your praises to the moon.

Be sure to post all your updates, but also post fun and interesting posts (not religious or political, nothing controversial), so people will genuinely like to follow you and post comments. Don't be a nonstop commercial. How many sites have you "unfollowed" because all they did was try to get you to buy something? But who doesn't like a cute animal clip? See how many likes and comments that gets.

Whatever social media you use, you need to interact at least a little, reposting their cute things, commenting here and there. Be a "real" person, not just a salesperson. If they feel like they "know" you, you have developed connections with real people, and real people read and buy books and leave reviews on Amazon.

Press Releases

Find out if your publisher sends out press releases to the big media news outlets. If they don't, you will need to do so. First, you will have to write a press release. It should contain a photo of your cover, a brief book blurb, a link to a free review copy, a link to a book trailer if you have one (and you should in this visual age), and a short bio. If you have a publisher that does press releases, ask them for a copy of it so you can send it to your local or more selective news media outlets, and post it in your media kit. If not, there are lots of examples and how-to's if you internet search how to write press releases for books.

You must then send out these releases to the news media. Here's a place to start with, that includes, a list of the top 100 media outlets: www.mondotimes.com/newspapers/usa/usatop100. There are also press distribution sites that will send your PR out for you, such as 24-7PressRelease.com (free release distribution with advertising support),1888PressRelease.com (free distribution, paid services gives you better placement and permanent archiving), NewswireToday.com (all the usual free distribution tools, premium service includes logo, product picture and more), PR.com (not only will this site distribute your press releases, but you can also set up a full company profile or your brand). There are many more distribution sites out there, so google away. Don't forget to send to your local news media yourself, even if your publisher sends out to the major networks. Email is the easiest way to reach editors these days. Send to TV, radio and newspapers. Offer to do an article, an interview, or a community spot.

Be sure to check your local PBS book stations and offer yourself up. It can be fun and exciting to do. After that first time, you will be a pro.

If you are intimidated by this and have the funds, you can hire a firm that specializes in this. Such a firm will send it out (or even write it) for you as it already has a list of recipients ready to go. Or, you can hire a publicist. A publicist will set up author readings, book signings, and other public appearances for you as well as send out to national and local news media groups. A publicist can, however, be pricy, so when just starting out you may have to do this yourself. Be prepared and know that once you create your lists, you can use them over and over, so they're valuable. Even if you hire someone else, eventually you need to know they are doing a good job, so it's best to understand the basics.

Conclusion

Well, you read the book on how to write a YA best seller. Think you can do it? The most important thing to remember from this book is writing YA is about teenagers, young people, kids on the cusp of adulthood. Get to know them. They're awesome, honest (for the most part), complicated people going through what must be the toughest time of their lives. Would you really want to be a teen today? Think what they face just going to school. Bullies, school shootings, friends on the brink of committing suicide, zits and raging hormones. And do it all over again? Bet you wouldn't. So, when you write about them, do it with compassion and soul. Feel what they feel, see through their eyes. It's the most important part of writing for teens.

You want to thrill them and engage them in your story, the one you're dying to tell. This book should help make writing that easier. It's about creating a story with characters that kids will believe in, making it come alive for them. That's the hard part.

If you plot your book using The Hero's Journey as detailed in Chapter Three, pick characters from the list in Chapter Six, put together a team filled with great sidekicks as detailed in Chapter Two, using archetypes and characters from Chapter Five and Six, you should have a great start.

Next, build a world using the information provided in Chapter Four, pick a time and setting using what you read in Chapter Eight, pace yourself through that sagging middle like you learned to do in Chapter Eleven, and head for a bonfire of an ending detailed in Chapter Twelve. Along the way give your characters some kick-butt dialogue as described in Chapter Ten. If you decide to make it a series, check out Chapter Thirteen. If you need tips for writing with a partner, it's in Chapter Sixteen.

This book is intended as an encyclopedia for writing Young Adult fiction. It is meant to help you from choosing what genre you want to write, to understanding what and why editors want certain things in the manuscripts they choose to champion. Keep this book where you can find it through the writing process as an easy reference to better understand how to develop rich, interesting characters to people the vivid, visual worlds you have learned to create. An award-winning YA author and an acquisitions editor/publisher sat down and wrote everything they thought you would need to help you through the process, no matter what writing experience or background you have. They honestly believe there's information between these covers that is helpful to writers of any fiction genre.

About the Author

Janet Schrader-Post

Daughter of a Colonel, Janet lived the military life until she got out of high school. At that point she was a self-described wild child. She got married and moved to Canada where she lived up the Sechelt Inlet, the scene for her YA novel, Spellcast Waters. She lived in a log cabin, with wood heat and a wood cook stove fifteen miles by boat from the nearest town. She's moved a lot. Between the military upbringing and just rambling around the country, she's moved 40 times. She understands settings.

She lived in Hawaii and worked as a polo groom for fifteen years, then moved to Florida where she became a reporter. For ten years she covered kids in high school and middle school. Kids as athletes, kids doing amazing things no matter how hard their circumstances. It impressed her, and it awed her. "How wonderful teens are. They have spirit and courage in the face of the roughest time of their lives. High school is a war zone. Between dodging bullies, school work and after school activities, teens nowadays have a lot on their plate. I wrote stories about them and I photographed them. My goal was to see every kid in their local newspaper before they graduated."

Janet love kids and horses, and she paints and writes. Now she lives in the swampland of Florida with too many dogs and her fifteen-year-old granddaughter. She started to write young adult fiction with the help of her son, Gabe Thompson, who teaches middle school. Together they wrote a young adult science fiction novel, which will eventually be a series, and have a middle grade book out, *Voodoo Child*, another, *My BFF is an Alien*, and one she wrote solo, *Spellcast Waters*. *Vagrant* was named a Finalist in the International Book Awards contest and was a Green Apple Special Selection winner.

Elizabeth "Doc E" Fortin-Hinds

Elizabeth believes in chasing dreams, and even makes dream catchers for friends. She's been a goal-setter her entire life and has a strong inner motivation to achieve them, no matter what conflicts she faces. She has lived a full and adventurous life and plans to keep those adventures coming, especially in books.

She knows kids well. She spent decades teaching teens and adults to write and improve their reading skills. As a literacy expert and certified coach, she helped both teachers from elementary to secondary and preservice graduate students learn to improve reading and writing instruction. She has taught at both the secondary and graduate level, everything from rhetoric, essays, and thesis statements, to poetry, short stories, and how to write a novel. She has learned to use both sides of her brain simultaneously, but enjoys the creative side the most, learning to play piano, draw and paint, and find time for her own writing since retiring from her "day" jobs.

A "true believer" in Joseph Campbell's *The Hero with a Thousand Faces*, mythic structures, she uses that lens when considering manuscripts for Tell-Tale Publishing Group, a company she founded with some friends from her critique group, upon retirement. That's where she earned the nickname, Doc E. With three doctors in the group of eight women, a dentist, an optometrist and a Ph.D. they were Doc C, Doc D and Elizabeth, Doc E.

She approached Janet, someone she considers to be one of the best authors of YA fiction, and a retired journalist so a prolific writer, to write this book because she saw a huge need for it and wanted to receive better YA submissions. Then, Janet, who has coauthored numerous books, countered with a request that Elizabeth coauthor. "Put your words where your mouth is," so here it is. Being a great negotiator, however, Elizabeth also convinced Janet, a marvelous artist as you can see, to draw the wonderful illustrations for this book. Elizabeth agreed to do one. Have fun finding it.

References

Albertalli, Becky. *The Upside of Unrequited*. First edition. New York, NY: Balzer + Bray, an imprint of HarperCollinsPublishers, 2017.

American Pie. Hollywood, CA: Universal, 2000.

Anderson, Laurie Halse. *Speak*. New York, N.Y.: Square Fish, 2011.

Aveyard, Victoria. *Red Queen*. First Edition. New York, NY: HarperTeen, an imprint of HarperCollins Publishers, 2015.

Back to the Future III. Directed by Robert Zemeckis, 1985.

Barry Eisler. Livia Lone. New York: Thomas & Mercer, 2016.

Beck, Christophe, et al. "*Waiting for Superman*", Hollywood, Calif.: Paramount Home Entertainment, 2011.

Bladerunner. Directed by Ridley Scott. Produced by Ridley Scott, 2007.

Bray, Libba., Erik Davies, and OverDrive Inc. *Going Bovine*. Unabridged. New York: Listening Library, 2009.

Campbell, Joseph. 2004. *The Hero with a Thousand Faces*. Princeton, N.J.: Princeton University Press.

Carroll, Lewis. *Alice's Adventures in Wonderland*. Strawberry Hills, N.S.W.: ReadHowYouWant Classics Library, 2016.

Carter, Thomas. Adler, Duane. Stiles, Julia. Thomas, Sean Patrick. Washington, Kerry. *Save the Last Dance*, Burbank, CA: Cort/Madden Productions, MTV Films, 2001.

Cass, Kiera. *The Elite*. New York: HarperTeen, 2013.

Child, Lincoln. How two writers can produce a novel together. Strand Magazine, Dec 2, 2015.

Claire Kann. Let's Talk About Love. New York: Swoon Reads, 2018.

Dahl, Roald, and Quentin Blake. *Matilda*. New York, N.Y., U.S.A.: Puffin, 1990.

Davis, Michael. Owen, Clive. Bellucci, Monica. Giamatti, Paul. *Shoot 'Em Up*. Angry Films. Burbank, CA: New Line Cinema, 2007.

Dexter: *The First Season, Volume 1*. Showtime, 2008.

Draanen, Wendelin Van. _Flipped. New York: Ember, 2016._

Elkels, Simone. Perfect Chemistry. New York, N.Y.: Walker Books, 2009.

Flynn, Gillian, 1971- author. Gone Girl : a Novel. New York: Crown, 2012.

Gaiman, Neil. Amano, Yoshitaka. The Sandman: The Dream Hunters. New York, N.Y.: Vertigo/D.C. Comics, 1999.

Gene Grant. King Geordi the Great. New York: Dreamspinner Press, 2014.

Green, John. _The Fault in Our Stars_. New York: Penguin Books USA, 2012.

Harris, Charlaine. Midnight Texas. New York, N.Y.: Penguin Publishing Group, 2014.

Hayes, Terry, George Miller, Doug Mitchell, George Ogilvie, Mel Gibson, and Tina Turner. 1991. _Mad Max: beyond Thunderdome._ Burbank, CA: Warner Home Video.

Herbert, Frank. _Dune_. Waterville, ME: Thorndike Press, a Part of Gale, Cengage Learning, 2015.

Hilton, James. Goodbye, Mr. Chips. New York, N.Y.: Hodder & Stoughton,

Hughes, Allen, Albert Hughes, Gary Whitta, Joel Silver, Denzel Washington, Broderick Johnson, Andrew A. Kosove, et al. 2010. _The Book of Eli._

Iliff, W. Peter, Tova Laiter, Michael Tollin, Brian Robbins, Mark Isham, James Van der Beek, Jon Voight, et al. 2009. _Varsity blues_. Hollywood, CA: Paramount Pictures.

Jemisine, N.K.. The Fifth Season. New York, N.Y.: Orbit, 2015.

Johnson, Dwayne. Gugino, Carla. Robb, Anna Sophia. Ludwig, Alexander, Harley, John. Burbank, CA: Walt Disney Studios Home Entertainment, 2009.

Keplinger, Kody. _The DUFF, Designated Ugly Fat Friend: A Novel_. New York: Little, Brown, 2010.

Kinney, Jeff. *Diary of a Wimpy Kid: Rodrick Rules*. Waterville, ME: Thorndike Press, a Part of Gale, Cengage Learning, 2017.

Kleiser, Randal, Bronté Woodard, Robert Stigwood, Allan Carr, Jim Jacobs, Warren Casey, John Travolta, et al. 2002.*Grease*.

Kong, Aleron. *The Land: Raiders*. Lexington, KY: CreateSpace Independent Publishing Platform, 2017.

Koontz, Dean. Odd Thomas. Reprint Edition. New York, N. Y.: Bantam, 2006.

MaCafferty, Megan. Jessica Darling's It List: The (Totally Not) Guaranteed Guide to Popularity, Prettiness & Perfection. New York, N.Y.: Poppy, 2013.

Marvel Studios presents a James Gunn film; co-producers, David J. Grant, Jonathan Schwartz; executive producers, Nik Korda, Stan Lee, Victoria Alonso, Jeremy Latcham, Alan Fine, Louis D'Esposito; produced by Kevin Feige; written by James Gunn and Nicole Perlman ; directed by James Gunn. Guardians of the Galaxy. [Burbank, California]: Marvel, 2014.

Meyer, Stephenie. Twilight. New York: Little, Brown and Co., 2005.

Millard, Nichole. Directed Fickman, Andy. Johnson, Dwayne. Burbank, CA: Buena Vista Pictures, 2007.

Mitchell, Saundra, Anna-Marie McLemore, Natalie C. Parker, Nilah Magruder, Mackenzi Lee, Robin Talley, Malinda Lo, Dahlia Adler, Kate Scelsa, Elliot Wake, Scott Tracey, Tess Sharpe, Alex Sanchez, Kody Keplinger, Sara Farizan, Tessa Gratton, Shaun David. Hutchinson, and Tehlor Kay. Mejia. *All Out: The No-longer-secret Stories of Queer Teens throughout the Ages*. Toronto, Ontario: Harlequin Teen, 2018.

Montgomery, R. A., Jason Millet, Sittisan Sundaravej, V. Pornkerd, S. Yaweera, J. Donploypetc, Gabhor Utomo, Laurence Peguy, Marco Cannella, T. Kornmaneeroj, K. Chanchaeron, S. Butsingkhon, and A. Utahigarn. *Choose Your Own Adventure Epic Collection*. Gosford, NSW: Scholastic Australia Pty, 2018.

Mos Eisley Cantina Pop-Up Book: Star Wars. New York, N.Y.: Little Brown & Co., 1995.

Murdock, Maureen. 1990. _The heroine's journey._ Boston, Mass: Shambhala.

Paolini, Christopher. _Eragon._ New York: Alfred A. Knopf, 2013.

Patterson, James. Tebbetts, Chris. Middle School: The Worst Years of My Life. New York, N.Y.: Little, Brown, 2011.

Post, Janet. Spellcast Waters. Swartz Creek, MI: Tell-Tale Publishing Group, LLC, 2018.

Post, Janet. Thompson, Gabe. My BFF is an Alien. Swartz Creek, MI: Tell-Tale Publishing Group, LLC, 2017.

Post, Janet. Thompson, Gabe. Voodoo Child. Swartz Creek, MI: Tell-Tale Publishing Group, LLC, 2018.

Riggs, Ransom. _Miss Peregrine's Home for Peculiar Children._ Philadelphia, PA: Quirk Books, 2011.

Riordan, Rick. _Percy Jackson and the Lightning Thief._ London: Puffin, 2006.

Ross, Gary, Stanley Tucci, Wes Bentley, Elizabeth Banks, Jennifer _Lawrence,_ Liam Hemsworth, and Suzanne Collins. 2012. _The hunger games._ [United States]: Alliance Film.

Roth, Veronica. _Divergent._ London: HarperCollins Publishers, 2016.

Roven, Charles, Richard Suckle, David Ayer, Will Smith, Jared Leto, Margot Robbie, Ike Barinholtz, Viola Davis, and David Harbour. 2016. _Suicide squad._

Rowling, J. K. _Harry Potter and the Chamber of Secrets._ New York: Scholastic, Inc., 2000.

Russo, Meredith. Meet Cute. New York, N.Y: HMH Books for Young Readers, 2018.

Sachar, Louis. Holes. New York: Yearling Books, 1998.

Sapphire. _Push: A Novel._ New York: Alfred A. Knopf, 1996.

Silver, Joel. Hughes, John. Hall, Anthony Michael. LeBrock, Kelly. Weird Science. Silver Pictures. Hughes Entertainment. Burbank, CA: Universal Pictures, 1985.

Spielberg, Steven, Chris Columbus, Harvey Bernhard, Richard Donner, Sean Astin, Josh Brolin, Jeff B. Cohen, et al. 2010. *The Goonies.* Burbank, Calif: Warner Bros. Entertainment, Inc.

The Bad News Bears. Chicago: Films Incorporated, 1976.

The Fifth Season by N.K. Jemisine

Thomas, Angie. The Hate You Give. New York, N,Y.: Balzer + Bray, an imprint of HarperCollins Publishers, 2017.

Thompson, Gabe. Vagrant. Swartz Creek, MI: Tell-Tale Publishing Group, LLC, 2016.

Tolkien, J. R. R. *The Lord of the Rings.* London: HarperCollins, 2016.

Touchstone Pictures. Brady, Tom. Schneider, John. D'Angelo, Carr. The Hot Chick. Happy Madison Productions, 2002.

Van Allsburg, Chris. *Jumanji.* Boston: Houghton Mifflin Co, 1981.

Vogler, Christopher. 1998. *The writer's journey: mythic structure for writers.* Studio City, CA: M. Wiese Productions.

Walt Disney Pictures presents in association with Jerry Bruckheimer Films a Technical Black production; a Boaz Yakin film; produced by Jerry Bruckheimer, Chad Oman; written by Gregory Allen Howard; directed by Boaz Yakin. Remember the Titans. Burbank, CA: Walt Disney Home Video: Distributed by Buena Vista Home Entertainment, 2007.

Walt Disney Pictures; produced by Walt Disney; story by Bill Peet; directed by Clyde Geronimi, Hamilton S. Luske, Wolfgang Reitherman; directing animator, Marc Davis ... [and others]. 101 Dalmatians. Burbank, Calif., Walt Disney Home Entertainment: Distributed by Buena Vista, 2008.

Waters, Mark S., Heather Hach, Leslie Dixon, Andrew Gunn, Jamie Lee Curtis, Lindsay Lohan, Mark Harmon, et al. 2003.*Freaky Friday.*

Waters, Mark S., Lorne Michaels, Louise Rosner, Tina Fey, Daryn Okada, Rolfe Kent, Wendy Greene Bricmont, et al. 2004. _Mean girls_.

Wegman, William, Carole Kismaric, and Marvin Heiferman. _Cinderella_. New York: Hyperion Books for Children, 1999.

Wilder, Laura Ingalls, 1867-1957. _Little House on the Prairie. New York, N.Y.: HarperCollins, 1992._

Woodson, Jacqueline. 1998. _If you come softly_.

Yancey, Richard. _The 5th Wave_. New York: G.P. Putnam's Sons, 2013.

Zemeckis, Robert, Michael Douglas, Kathleen Turner, Danny DeVito, _Zack Norman_, Alfonso Arau, Manuel Ojeda, Jack Brodsky, Joel Douglas, and Diane Thomas. 2006. _Romancing the stone_. Beverly Hills, Calif: 20th Century Fox Home Entertainment.

CPSIA information can be obtained
at www.ICGtesting.com
Printed in the USA
LVHW011916271118
598388LV00012B/347/P